Canadian Pacific

Canadian Pacific

Jim Lotz

Bison Books

Published by
Bison Book Ltd.
176 Old Brompton Road,
London, SW 5
England.

ISBN 0 86124 216 5

Printed in Hong Kong

Page 1: Engine 1407 takes *The Canadian* round the bend of a fast-flowing trout
stream which winds its way undisturbed out of the Canadian Rockies.
Page 2-3: Engine 5006, in 'action red' markings, and a yellow Canadian Pacific
caboose idle in the snow near Smith Falls, Ontario on a crisp, chilly New Year's Day
in 1981.
Below: This view of a stainless steel domed observation car of *The Canadian* dates
from 1968, before VIA Rail took over the operation of all Canadian passenger
service.

Acknowledgements

I'd like to thank my wife, Pat, for her help. The Public Relations people at
Canadian Pacific provided a great deal of useful information very promptly,
and were extremely helpful. I'd also like to acknowledge the help of the
Halifax City Regional Library. They proved yet again what a treasure trove
of knowledge a public library can be for a writer.

The author and publisher would like to thank the following people who
have helped in the preparation of this book: Bill Yenne, who designed it
and did the picture research; Thomas G Aylesworth, who edited it; Rod
Baird who prepared the index and wrote the captions.

Picture Credits

Unless otherwise specified all photos are credited to the Canadian Pacific Archives:

Fred Angus 7
Burlington Northern Railway 20-21 (both)
Canada Postal Corporation 15 (above)
Canadian Broadcasting Corporation 26-27, 30
Canadian National Railway 73 (top)
Canadian Pacific (via Jim Lotz) 127 (bottom)
Glenbow Archives, Calgary, Alberta 24-25, 31, 58-59, 66-67, 69, 70-71
Colin K Hatcher 8-9, 108-109 (both), 116 (top), 117 (bottom)
Jim Hope 59 (top)
Vic R Reyna 2-3, 106-107, 110-111, 114-115 (bottom left and right)
Stan F Styles 4-5, 12, 49, 51 (top), 53 (top), 56-57 (bottom), 61, 64-65 (bottom),
72-73 (bottom), 74-75 (all), 76-77 (top left, bottom both), 78 (top both), 81 (both),
82-83 (both), 86-87, 88-89, 90-91, 125
Via Rail Canada 112-113
© **Bill Yenne** 114-115 (top), 118-119 (top)

Contents

The CPR — A Peculiarly Canadian Institution

'Institutions, like technology, are materializations of the fantasies of a past generation, inflicted on the present.'
Philip Slater, *The Pursuit of Loneliness*

The Canadian Pacific Railway turned Canada from a notion into a nation.

When the last spike of the railway was driven at Craigellachie, about 30 miles west of Revelstoke, British Columbia, on 7 November, 1885, Canada gained a new sense of identity and new world image.

The railway began with the vision of a politician who was blissfully unaware of the enormous financial, physical and political difficulties involved in tying together the scattered bits of Canada. The terms of agreement under which Sir John A Macdonald brought British Columbia into Confederation in 1871-72 specified:

The Government of the Dominion undertake to secure the commencement simultaneously, within two years from the date of union, of the construction of a railway from the Pacific towards the Rocky Mountains, and from such point as may be selected east of the Rocky Mountains towards the Pacific, to connect the seaboard of British Columbia with the railway system of Canada; and further, to secure completion of such railway within ten years from the date of union.

It's hard now to appreciate the sense of achievement and pride that marked the completion of the Canadian Pacific Railway. The railway has been called 'a national necessity,' 'the national dream,' 'the wedding band of Confederation,' Canadian capitalism's 'proudest product' and 'The Domination of Canada on wheels.' It became a clue in a Sherlock Holmes story, and Baroness Orczy dedicated a romantic novel to: 'The President, Directors and all connected with that magnificent organization . . .' E J Pratt wrote a poem entitled *Towards the Last Spike* which had the line: 'A western version of the Arctic daring/Romance and realism, double dose.' Frank Underhill, a pioneer socialist, once suggested

that Canada's greatest need was for 'a moral equivalent of the CPR.'

The railway has always had about it a touch of magnificence and majesty, a blend of rightness and righteousness. The modest last spike ceremony ended a great endeavour on a low key. But the plaque that marks the site of the ceremony reads like poetry:

A nebulous dream was a reality: an iron ribbon crossed Canada from sea to sea. Often following the footsteps of early explorers, nearly 3000 miles of steel rail pushed across vast prairies, cleft lofty mountain passes, twisted through canyons, and bridged a thousand streams.

Here on Nov. 7, 1885, a plain iron spike welded East to West.

Myth and legend cling to the railway. Walter Moberly, searching for a pass through the mountains in 1865, shot at an eagle's nest, and watched the birds fly into a river valley. Eagle Pass carries the railway line through the mountains, following the route of these birds. The Connaught Tunnel, which carries the line through Rogers Pass, is reported to be the home of sightless mice which live on grain spilled from the passing hopper cars.

The railway linked the cities of eastern Canada and the empty lands of the west in the 19th century. Then, during the 20th century, the line took people away from these lands, to war and the cities of the east. The CPR soon became the one Canadian institution that non-Canadians had heard about — apart from the Mounties. Both quickly gained a reputation for excellence, reliability and dedication to service.

To eastern Canadians, the CPR represented progress and civilization penetrating an empty wilderness. But to westerners, the railway soon became visible evidence of eastern domination and exploitation. When the CPR built its

Windsor Station, Montreal, Québec 6 November 1960. The last remaining CPR steam train completes its last run. An era has ended.

line through the Crowsnest Pass into southern British Columbia at the end of the last century, it received government grants. In return, it agreed to keep the freight charges on western grain at a low rate. This 'Crow Rate' became a symbol of regional relationship, a topic of conversation on the prairies, and a fundamental element in the culture of western families. A joke tells of a prairie farmer arriving home to find his crop flattened by hail, his barn on fire, and his wife running away with the hired hand. He looks up to Heaven, and shouts; 'Goddam the CPR!'

Thus the great national venture aimed at uniting Canada soon began to divide it. As the Canadian Pacific became larger, its very success and bigness was seen as a threat by Canadians. A journalist writing a book on the Company was asked by a former mayor of Vancouver – a city created by the Canadian Pacific – whether she was going to call it *CP: Good Guys or Bad Guys?* A radical writer called his book *The CPR: A Century of Corporate Welfare.* Like many other left-wingers, he believed that the CPR should be nationalized. But he reserved his harshest criticism for officials of the government of Canada, presumably for helping the CPR to become so successful and profitable, not for the Company's officers.

The railway was built through the sort of partnership and compromise between government and the private sector that is peculiarly Canadian. Macdonald knew that the government could not build the railway to the Pacific. It had tried and failed. And the members of the Syndicate who came together to bid for the contract for the line knew that they could not carry it off alone. The CPR had to please the politicians and the public – and make a profit. So a private/government

partnership developed – as did a love/hate relationship between the two parties.

Railways are more than steam and steel and balance sheets. They arouse deep emotions in people. The CPR locomotives, concrete embodiments of progress, hauling luxurious passenger trains and heavy freight trains, became a fixed feature in the lives of westerners until other transcontinental lines were completed. Then these lines went broke, and the government took them over and ran them at a loss. But the CPR steamed on.

It's still possible to catch something of what the railways meant in the past as you travel by train across the prairies. Golden and green in summer, black and white in winter, the land stretches to the endless horizon. At night, pinpoints of light mark the small communities, and a sudden flash of neon the larger ones along the railway. The grain elevators loom along the line like giant elephants asleep. On the sidings, the blue hopper cars are labelled 'Heritage Fund,' for they have been paid for by the Conservative government of Alberta. The red ones, paid for by a Liberal federal government, carry the words 'Government of Canada.' The trains bring a flash of moving light and colour into an ageless land tamed now for agriculture.

The steam train, once welcomed or feared as a harbinger of a new industrial order and way of life, has now become an object of romantic nostalgia, a reminder of the good old days.

I came from a railwayman's family, and have no nostalgia for the days of steam. My father worked as a baggage attendant at a station in Britain. He did three eight-hour shifts, on a rotating basis, so that the baggage room could be open round the clock. He had one Sunday off every three weeks. During the Second World War, he cycled to work through the air raids on Liverpool, shaking with malaria picked up during the First World War. He did not do so for love of the railway

CPR's *The Canadian,* Train No. 1 'Sibley Park' halts in Swift Current,
Saskatchewan on a chilly November day in 1977. *The Canadian* crosses the
continent from Montreal to Vancouver, a total of 3045 miles, by rail.

company, or for the convenience of its passengers. He did so from a sense of loyalty to his fellow-workers. He remained in the same job until he retired, never earning much money, but knowing he had a steady job and a steady wage that would support his family.

And that was the attraction for many railway workers in Canada, especially those employed by the CPR. They earned a decent wage – and enjoyed the status that came with working for a large, powerful and successful company.

Over the last two decades, the Canadian Pacific has become concerned about its image. An academic who wrote a commissioned book on the Company in 1968 stated: 'A great many attitudes towards the Company were built up in those early years of strain and difficulty which took on a life of their own and created unnecessary difficulties in later years.'

The concept of corporate culture offers a way of understanding and appreciating the story of the CPR. Those who work for a large company, like members of an isolated tribe, develop a set of attitudes, values, beliefs and expectations. The CPR began with an enormous burst of energy and idealism, fuelled by the desire to serve the national interest in Canada – and to make a profit. The Company kept growing, but as it had to run more and more transportation systems, it had to regulate its affairs to ensure that trains and ships left on time. Thus bureaucratization slowed down the initial energetic thrust. The Company had a series of strong-minded presidents who combined innovative thrusts with the ability to delegate responsibility so that things kept moving.

Like an isolated tribe, the Company has erected its monuments, created its folk heroes and spawned myths and legends. One of its viaducts near Lethbridge, Alberta, a high level steel bridge, 'straight dark line of metal drawn against

the prairie sky,' has been elevated to an art object by a writer in a national newspaper. He describes the towers 'which shoulder their burden with the perfect simplicity and athletic grace characteristic of all great twentieth-century engineering.' And so they do.

This Canadian corporation came into being through the efforts of thrifty Scottish entrepreneurs and American railway builders. The labour force came from the farms of the Dakotas and Manitoba, the cities of the east – and the fields of China. Men like George Stephen, Donald Smith, William Van Horne, Sandford Fleming and others have passed into Canadian history books as prime examples of 19th century capitalists and engineers. Others who worked for the CPR remain in the shadow. Kate Reed decorated the Company's hotels with quiet elegance and good taste. Tom Wilson, a western guide, helped the early explorers, surveyors and railway builders. John Murray Gibbon did much to preserve and encourage the culture of Canada before government discovered it. And there are countless others who worked on the railway and have stories to tell.

The Company had to balance two sets of forces – those pushing it towards innovation and expansion, and those pulling it towards contraction so that its resources were not over-extended. To balance these tensions, the CPR established standards of excellence and adopted the newest technology. When it realized that big was no longer beautiful, it broke up into scores of small profit centres. It weathered the depression of the early 1980s, although some of its operations proved to be 'loss centres.' The railway continued to turn a profit when the ships and planes lost money. In the first six months of 1984, CP rail freight tonnage rose by 11.7 percent over the previous year. The profits of Canadian

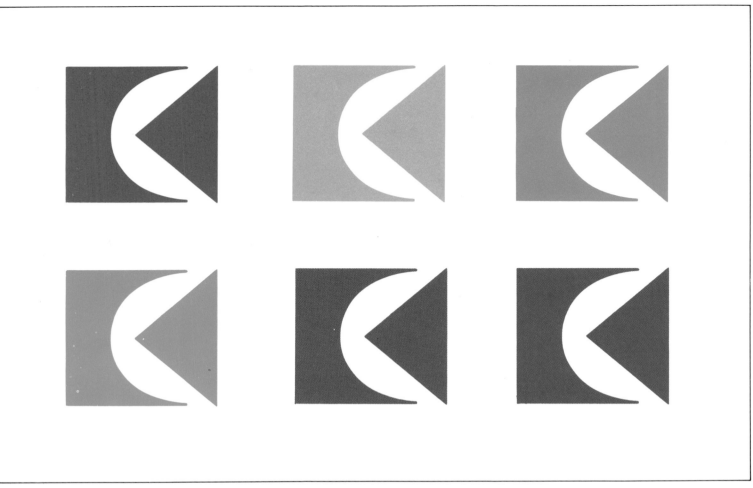

Pacific Enterprises Ltd, the organization that operates the non-transportation sections of Canadian Pacific, increased from $10.8 million in the first six months of 1983 to $125.4 million for the same period in 1984. The size of the Company's operations remains awesome. It plans to spend $7.6 billion in the 1980s.

As the government begins to see private enterprise as the saviour of Canada, the Canadian Pacific has bounced back from the recession in fighting shape. In 1983, the Company hired Donald Colussy, former president of Pan-American Airways, to run CP Air. In June 1984, the airline issued a special four-page advertising supplement headed 'Customer Service is CP Air's Ace.' Colussy was quoted as saying: 'We're looking at increased competition as an opportunity' as the government talked about deregulating the airline industry.

In the same month, Frederick Burbidge, president of the Canadian Pacific, told shareholders at the Company's annual meeting: 'Business should rely on its own initiative and stop crying for government help whenever it gets into trouble of its own making.' The Company had tried to put down a code of ethics on paper, he told another audience, and ended up with a 19 page document. Burbidge cited the head of another international company who had advised him: 'My code of conduct is very simple. Don't do anything you can't explain on television.'

Men like Stephen and Van Horne were never concerned about their image. They knew that the secret of success for any business lay in pleasing the customer.

The company they created remains a great Canadian achievement – and ranks with the world's best run and most successful businesses.

Facing page: The original CPR logo, adopted in July 1886, simply carried the company's name on an ornate shield. In December of the same year, the shield was simplified and the beaver was added at the top. When the logo was being developed, the Company's founders felt that the industrious beaver was symbolic of their image of Canadian Pacific.

Over the years the shield went through several permutations and ultimately became a good deal more simplified. The slogans 'World's Greatest Travel System' and 'Spans The World' were put into use during the early years of the century and were used in the Company's advertising. In both cases the slogans reflected the Company's activities in shipping and eventually aviation, as well as in railroading.

By World War II, script lettering came into use. In 1946, after World War II, the shield was further simplified to the simple red form at lower left. The red and white checked flag (originally designed by Van Horne) was adopted for the Company's steamships and the Canada Goose for Canadian Pacific Airlines (established in 1942). The Company name in script lettering was used on the sides of the Company's vehicles, from locomotives to airplanes. Several examples of this usage are seen at various places in this book.

Above: The Company's present, severely stylized logos were adopted amid a good deal of fanfare in 1968. They are used along with the names of the Company's six components which are set in the typeface known as Helvetica Bold Italic.

The names of the Company's various components were also shortened and stylized. The logos in the top row are red for CP Rail (formerly Canadian Pacific Railway), orange for CP Air (formerly Canadian Pacific Airlines) and green for CP Ships. The bottom row features blue for CP Transport, gray for CP Hotels and brown for the CP Telecommunications component.

This color coding carries over into the color scheme of the Company's vehicles. For example, CP Rail locomotives are usually red, CP Air airliners are usually orange and CP Transport's trucks are predominantly blue. In use on company vehicles, the triangle is usually in black within a white half-circle, with the rest of the vehicle painted the appropriate color.

(See page 89.)

A Vision of Unity

'Many in this room will live to hear the whistle of the steam-engine in the passes of the Rocky Mountains and to make the journey from Halifax to the Pacific in five or six days.'
Joseph Howe, 1851

On 10 May 1869, a railway president swung a hammer to drive in the last spike on a railway line linking the Atlantic and Pacific Oceans – and missed.

Then Leland Stanford tried again, tapping home the gold spike that linked the Union Pacific and the Central Pacific railways at Promontory Point in Utah. This small noise in the wilderness echoed through the corridors of power in London and Ottawa, making politicians there nervous about the expansion of the United States. The restless Americans, who had ceased to expend their energies in a civil war, were now heading west to open up the frontier beyond the Mississippi. British and Canadian politicians worried that the Americans, fired by their belief in 'manifest destiny,' might move north, settle the prairies and demand annexation by their government.

Canada had come into being in 1867 as a Confederation of Ontario, Quebec, New Brunswick and Nova Scotia; British Columbia remained a colonial province. Between it and Canada lay two large chunks of territory – Rupert's Land, the domain of the Hudson's Bay Company, and the North-Western Territory, a British possession. 'Canada would break off in the middle unless we linked it up with a steel rail' was how one westerner put the new nation's problem. In 1871, Canada had only 23,000 of its population of 3½ million living west of Lake Superior; wandering Indians following the buffalo, Métis creating a new society on the Red River, fur traders, gold miners, and a few restless souls occupied the empty land between the Great Lakes and the mountains. The United States had bought Alaska from Russia in 1867. If it acquired British Columbia, it would have a land link to the new territory and cut Canada off from access to the Pacific coast. If Americans also took over the prairies, the new nation would lose its hinterland.

Internal revolt as well as external domination threatened the backyard of the four provinces. In 1870, Canada acquired Rupert's Land and the North-Western Territory. In the previous year, the Métis, threatened by the expansion of settlers into their lands, had risen under Louis Riel. Sir John A Macdonald, the Prime Minister, sent the Red River Expedition under a British soldier to suppress the rebellion. But he also negotiated with the westerners, and on 15 July 1870, the province of Manitoba came into being. In the following year,

CPR conquered Canada's mountains and exposed their scenic beauty for all to see. Mt Cathedral looms over Cathedral Station in 1949.

Sir John lured British Columbia into Confederation with the promise of a railway to the Pacific.

On the same day that the sixth province joined Canada, a survey party set out from Victoria, its capital, to locate a route for the railway line. The first railway surveyors from the east had left Ottawa about five weeks earlier. In the 1850s 'Railway mania' had swept Canada, and a rash of lines had been constructed to serve local needs. In 1861, the Grand Trunk Railway, built to channel the American western trade into the St Lawrence, went bankrupt with debts of $13 million. After Confederation, Macdonald committed the federal government to completing an Intercolonial Railway to link the networks of Ontario and Quebec with those of New Brunswick and Nova Scotia. That railway opened on 15 July 1876, having cost almost twice the estimated amount.

The gold spike that completed the American interocean line bore a prayer: 'May God continue the unity of our country as this Railroad unites the two great Oceans of the World.' Macdonald knew that he could not rely on the Almighty, nor on unbridled capitalism, to build a railway to the Pacific. The construction of railway lines in the United States had been marked by graft and corruption, haste and waste. Dummy companies built the lines, and entrepreneurs skimmed off millions in government money provided for their construction. They had little interest in operating the railways. Passengers had to change trains to cross the continent, and suffered many other discomforts. When Leland Stanford drove home his last spike, three companies of infantry stood by with fixed bayonets. The Indians had resisted the railway and been subdued by force. When the trains began to run, they attacked them and attempted to lasso the iron horse.

Macdonald wanted more than just two ribbons of steel across the empty west and through the mountains. He wanted an instrument of national unity, and an opportunity to serve the needs of the British Empire.

A road from Halifax to the Fraser River had been proposed by a British writer in 1849 '. . . to link up the whole English race, and to furnish Great Britain a soil for her population and a market for her labour.' The road could be built for £150 million by convicts and Indians, with the help of local labour. In 1850, A B Richards, another British visionary, promoted the same idea in *British Redeemed and Canada Preserved*.

The arrival of Joseph Whitehead's first locomotive at Winnipeg on 9 October 1877 was a cause for celebration. The presence of a locomotive, the first one on the Canadian prairies, enabled tracklaying to begin on the Pembina Branch. The sternwheeler *Selkirk* pushed a barge laden with the locomotive, conductor's van and six flatcars. The barge is grounded against the muddy riverbank. Flags flap in the fall river breezes as the sternwheeler's crew and deckhands pose for their picture on the third flatcar, to the left of the tender. Note that the name Canadian Pacific appears on the equipment, though the CPR company was still three-and-a-half years in the future. The locomotive, the *Countess of Dufferin*, is now on display in Winnipeg.

His scheme involved using 20,000 convicts, guarded by 5000 men and aided by 6000 able-bodied paupers. Joseph Howe had visited Britain in 1850 to seek funding for a railway to link the Maritimes with Upper Canada, and come back with visions of steam whistles blowing in the Rockies and of a journey from Halifax to the Pacific of only five or six days. In 1857, an Imperial Commission inquired into the 'suitability of the colony of Canada for settlement and the advisability of constructing a transcontinental line of railway.'

The North West Transportation, Navigation and Railway Company, established in 1858, proposed to connect points in the interior with the rest of Canada, but little came of its dreams and schemes. Three years later, E W Watkins of the Grand Trunk Railway tried to secure the co-operation of the Hudson's Bay Company in building a telegraph line and a common highway between Canada and the Pacific. The idea sent one governor of the Company into hysterics; 'What! Sequester our very tap roots! Take away the fertile lands where our buffalo feed! Let in all kinds of people to squat and settle and frighten away the fur-bearing animals they don't kill and hunt. Impossible!'

By 1870, the only land link between Canada and the West was the Dawson Route, a rough wagon road built in 1870 from the head of Lake Superior to the Red River settlement to speed up the passage of troops to suppress the first Riel uprising. A few hundred settlers trickled into Manitoba along this route. But most people went west by first going south, using the American railways, and then heading north up the Red River Valley to Winnipeg.

In 1870, Macdonald wrote to T C Brydges, manager of the Grand Trunk Railway: 'It is quite evident to me from advices from Washington, that the United States Government are resolved to do all they can, short of war, to get possession of the western territory, and we must take immediate and vigorous steps to counteract them. One of the first things to be done is to show unmistakeably our resolve to build the Pacific Railway.'

Macdonald had never visited the west. His promise to link British Columbia with the rest of Canada had been made in blithe ignorance of the financial and physical difficulties involved. Gold created British Columbia – and an impatient people who wanted quick action on Macdonald's promise of a railway. In other places, the transcontinental railway was being dismissed as an impossible dream. One old judge snorted that Macdonald had 'gone clean crazy . . . the next thing he will be talking about a railway to the moon . . .'

The politicians in Ottawa had received widely differing reports on the west. The British officer who led the Palliser Expedition in the late 1850s reported that the west was a desert and the Rockies impassable: 'The knowledge of the country, on the whole, would never lead me to advocate a line of communication from Canada across the continent to the Pacific, exclusively through British territory. The time has now forever gone by for effecting such an object.' Two Canadian travellers, Simon J Dawson and Henry Youle Hinds, reported more favorably about the potential of the land between the American border and the boreal forests. But the west's first truly enthusiastic supporter was John Macoun.

Macoun, a self-taught naturalist, joined Sandford Fleming's exploring party in 1872. Fleming, who had completed the survey of the Intercolonial Railway in 1869, had overall direction of the transcontinental one. Macoun applied his boundless enthusiasm and energy to its cause. He reported that Palliser's 'conclusions regarding the passes through the mountains were as accurate as his conclusions regarding the lands.' Fleming's survey located the line to the north of Lake Superior, across the northern prairies and through the Yellowhead Pass down to tidewater on the Pacific. Since most Canadian voters in British Columbia lived in and around Victoria, one route included a bridge over the Seymour Narrows to Vancouver Island, and thence to that city. Fleming estimated the cost of the railway at around $100 million.

Macdonald granted federal charters to two private companies in 1872. The Canadian Pacific Railway Company, headed by Sir Hugh Allan, a shipowner and one of the wealthiest men in Canada, consisted mainly of Montreal interests. A competing group, the Inter-Ocean Railway Company, headed by D L MacPherson and associated with the Grand Trunk Railway, also received a charter. Macdonald tried to merge the two groups, but the Toronto company objected because Allan's backers included Americans.

After the election in August 1872, from which Macdonald emerged victorious, Allan agreed to exclude the American interests. The Prime Minister promised his company a new charter, a subsidy of $30 million and 50 million acres of land. Someone then leaked correspondence revealing that Allan had given Macdonald $300,000 to help him to win the 1872 election. The 'Pacific Scandal' erupted, some of his party

abandoned Macdonald and he was forced to call another election, which he lost.

The Liberals under Alexander Mackenzie, a dour stonemason, took office in 1874. The new Prime Minister decided to build the transcontinental line in bits and pieces, linking up waterways in the west with short pieces of track. Money was short, but time was not. Mackenzie dismissed the 1881 deadline for the completion of the line to British Columbia, claiming in 1875 that '. . . all the power of men and all the money in Europe could not likely complete the Pacific railway in ten years.'

Right: The locomotive which started it all, CPR No 1, is lovingly maintained and displayed in Winnipeg, Manitoba. It is named *Countess of Dufferin* after the wife of the then Governor-General who was in Winnipeg on the day the locomotive arrived. In the inset, the famous locomotive is commemorated by a Canadian 32 cent stamp.

During Mackenzie's administration, work on the line continued in a desultory manner, with the government hiring contractors to build sections of track. An attempt was made to turn the Dawson route into a railway, the first sod on this part of the line being turned on 1 June 1875, near what is now the city of Thunder Bay. Rock, forest and muskeg severely hampered the railway builders as the line slowly advanced.

The first locomotive in the Canadian west arrived by barge in Winnipeg on 9 October 1877. Its owner, Joseph Whitehead, named it *Countess of Dufferin,* in honour of the wife of the Governor-General who was in the city when the barge arrived. It carried on its side the proud designation 'CPR No. 1' and the tender and the rolling stock bore the words 'Canadian Pacific.'

The vision of a transcontinental railway remained alive.

Monsignor Taché, the Catholic Archbishop of Winnipeg, wrote early in 1878 that rails had been laid 25 miles to the north and east, and an embankment completed south to Pembina. Next fall, he had been told, it would be possible to take a train from a mile from the Cathedral and reach Montreal in a few days, changing only at Chicago: 'O tempora! . . . Would you have believed it?'

Countess of Dufferin 4-4-0 type / Countess of Dufferin type 4-4-0

The Team

'Nothing is too small to know, and nothing too big to attempt.'
William Cornelius Van Horne's maxim

In October, 1878, Macdonald and his Conservatives swept back into power.

The Prime Minister made the completion of a transcontinental railway part of his National Policy. Much more was now known about the west as a result of the railway surveys. Passes had been found through the Rockies, and red fife wheat was yielding 25 bushels an acre in Manitoba. In 1877, the irrepressible John Macoun, 'cautioned, in plain words, not to draw upon my imagination,' had written a report for the government identifying 80 million acres of arable land and 120 million acres of pasture, swamp and lakes in the west.

When Macdonald introduced his Railway Bill into Parliament in 1879, the Liberal Opposition attacked the 'road from Ocean to Ocean.' Manitoba was dismissed as 'little more than a bog or marsh.' At one point, Macoun joined in the debate from the gallery, suggesting that Opposition leader Mackenzie read his report. A royal commission on the government's attempts to build a transcontinental line reported in 1880 that the 'construction of the Canadian Pacific Railway was carried on as a Public Work at a sacrifice of money, time and efficiency.'

Macdonald, a tired man, had seen his vision of national unity divide the country and his dream of a transcontinental railway become a nightmare. He tried to interest British investors in his scheme, with no success. Then, in the spring of 1880, he received an offer from a group of Montreal entrepreneurs. It included George Stephen, president of the Bank of Montreal, R B Angus, its former general manager, Donald Smith, chief commissioner of the Hudson's Bay Company, James J Hill, a railway builder and Duncan McIntyre, who controlled the Canada Central Railway.

George Stephen, son of a carpenter, was born in northeastern Scotland in 1829. Early in life he had been told by his mother 'that I must aim at being a thorough master of the work by which I had to get my living, and to be that I must concentrate . . . my whole energies on my work . . . to the exclusion of every other thing.' Leaving school at 14, Stephen had been apprenticed to a draper and silk mercer in Aberdeen before moving to Canada in 1850. There he became a successful entrepreneur in the dry goods, wool and cotton industries and a member of Montreal's commercial and social four hundred.

His cousin, Donald Smith, had served the Hudson's Bay Company on the coast of Labrador. In this tough training ground for traders, he had not been blinded by the Bay's traditional view of the west as a pristine wilderness for fur-bearers and Indians. He knew that the prosperity of his company and of Canada lay in peopling the prairies with settlers.

Stephen and Smith had seen how railways had opened up the American West. In the early 1870s, they had applied to build railway lines from the American border to Fort Garry, and from Prince Arthur's Landing on Lake Superior to Fort Garry.

As the Canadian economy stagnated through the 1870s, the idea of a transcontinental railway as a catalyst for development became attractive to Canadian capitalists. The *Montreal Journal of Commerce* of 19 October 1877 lamented: 'Money, floating capital, unused funds, are more abundant than ever; the cash-boxes overflow; the large banks literally sweat with gold; and this excess, this plethora of unemployed capital, causes the public funds to advance and the price of money to decrease. It is business that is wanting; it is the employment of capital that is in default . . .'

George Stephen believed that a railway would bring western wheat to the world through the ports of the St Lawrence, and take manufactured goods to the prairies to supply the settlers who would pour into this empty land. His business vision complemented the political one of Macdonald, and Stephen played the leading role in moving the Canadian Pacific Railway from an idea and a few stretches of track towards a reality.

The group (or Syndicate as it became known) had recently rescued the St Paul and Pacific Railway, which speculators, grasshoppers, unfriendly Indians and a lack of traffic had forced into receivership in the 1870s. In 1879, Stephen recalled the misery he had suffered during the ten years he had worked to secure control of the line (renamed the St Paul, Minneapolis and Manitoba Railway) and turn it into a profitable venture. But, he added, 'what maun [must] be maun be.'

Right: Cornelius Van Horne, a large man of large appetites, a nineteenth century capitalist of mythic proportions, was general manager of the CPR. His drive and organizing skills took CPR across the continent.

Donald Smith, who represented a Manitoba riding in Parliament, had earned Macdonald's mistrust by bolting Conservative ranks during the Pacific Scandal. Stephen bore the main burden of dealing with the Prime Minister and finding the funds to build the railway.

As negotiations over the building of the line proceeded, Stephen wrote to Macdonald that 'my friends and my enemies agree that the venture will be the ruin of us all.'

The Prime Minister needed a group of people who could operate a transcontinental line as well as building it.

The Syndicate, now enjoying profits from the St Paul, Minneapolis and Manitoba Railway, drove a hard bargain with the government, requesting a subsidy of $26.5 million and 35 acres of land. The contract with the government gave the Canadian Pacific Railway Company $25 million in cash and 25 million acres of land ('fairly fit for settlement'), exemption from taxes, and the promise that no other railway would be built south of the main line west of Lake Superior for 20 years. Introduced into Parliament on 9 December 1880, the Railway Bill became law on 15 February 1881, and the Canadian Pacific Railway charter was issued on the following day. The Syndicate put down a $1 million cheque as security, and the new company held its first meeting on 17 February 1881.

The new railway also received over 710 miles of line already contracted for or completed, including the section between Port Arthur and Selkirk, near Winnipeg; a link between Selkirk and Emerson on the American border and the section from Kamloops to Port Moody in British Columbia.

The seemingly endless prairie stretching west from Winnipeg to the foothills of the Rockies was patrolled by the North West Mounted Police. Created in 1873, this force had moved into the vacuum left when the Hudson's Bay Company gave up its lands to Canada. The Mounties brought peace to the west, evicted American whiskey traders, and made contact with the Indians. But the vanishing buffalo and the starvation years that followed made the Indians restive. No one knew how they would react to the coming of the powerful symbols of central Canadian domination. In the United States, 5000 troops had protected the first transcontinental line.

A competent American engineer, Andrew Onderdonk, had a $9.1 million contract to build 127 miles of track between Yale and Kamloops. From there the line would head northeast through the Yellowhead Pass and slice across the prairies along the route surveyed by Sandford Fleming. In all, the transcontinental line would stretch for 2600 miles between Callander and Port Moody on the Pacific, and the new company would have to build 1900 miles of this.

James Hill, short, bandy-legged, barrel-chested and one-eyed, took charge of the construction. He appointed Alpheus Stickney of the St Paul, Minneapolis and Manitoba Railway as superintendent of construction, and made Thomas A Rosser, a former Confederate general, chief engineer. He also sent Major A B Rogers to find a route through the Rockies south of the Yellowhead.

Accompanied by his brother and ten Indian packers carrying 100 pounds each, the peppery 'master of picturesque profanity' plunged into the mountains in 1881. The Company had promised that they would name the pass he found after him, and pay him a $5000 bonus. In 1882 he discovered a route through the Selkirks. When first he saw Rogers Pass, he exclaimed: 'Hell's bells, ain't that a pretty sight!'

Facing page: George Stephen was the first president of CPR, 1881-1888. *Above:* Donald A Smith was Stephen's cousin, a former Hudson's Bay Company trader who envisioned CPR's role in the future commerce of Canada.

In negotiations with Macdonald, the Company had stated that it 'should expect to be allowed to locate the line as we would think proper.' Hill hoped the transcontinental line would bypass the rough terrain north of Lake Superior and connect with the St Paul, Minneapolis and Manitoba Railway and a line that he controlled between St Paul and the Sault. This idea proved unpalatable to Stephen and Macdonald who wanted an all-Canadian route. Hill left the Syndicate in May 1883, swearing to build his own railway to the Pacific. He completed the Great Northern Railway, the fifth American transcontinental line, on 3 January 1893 – without a grant of land or government loan. Hill became a thorn in the Company's side, continually trying to divert traffic south of the border.

The railway generated a land boom in Winnipeg in the early 1880s, as speculators poured into town, and local people expected instant wealth from the sale of land to settlers.

Stickney and Rosser became more interested in making money from speculation than in pushing ahead with the railway. Hill invited 38-year-old William Cornelius Van Horne, General Superintendent of the Chicago, Milwaukee and St Paul Railway, to visit Winnipeg in 1881 to examine the progress of the line. When this remarkable man returned to town on Christmas Day of that year, and took over as general manager of the CPR on 2 January 1882, things began moving.

Born in 1843, Van Horne left school at 14, and became a telegraph operator. Railways, the high technology of their time, offered ambitious young men a way to the top. Railways had made Van Horne – and he made the CPR. While George Stephen retained absolute control of the Company, Van Horne took all the power he could to build the line. When completed, it was known for years as 'Van Horne's Line.'

The *Winnipeg Sun* claimed that 'Van Horne is calm and harmless-looking. So is a she-mule; and so is a buzz-saw.' David Hanna, first president of Canadian National Railways, wrote in 1926 that 'Among the Grand Trunk wise men, the enterprise that was poking its nose into the barbarian wilderness was looked upon with an almost amused toleration . . . The CPR was very much a colonial affair, don't you know – indeed with a general manager from Milwaukee, rather too Yankee an affair . . .'

But Hanna described Van Horne's approach to railway building as 'the most remarkable innovation that has happened in the business life of the Dominion . . . His vocabulary had all the certainty that belonged to the Presbyterian conception of everlasting retribution, without its restraints. He laughed at other men's impossibilities, and ordered them to be done – a dynamo run by dynamite.'

Van Horne himself dismissed sleep as merely a habit, and said: 'I eat all I can, I drink all I can, I smoke all I can, and I don't give a damn for anything.' When an engineer refused to take a locomotive across a difficult place, Van Horne ordered him out of the cab, and prepared to take the train across. The engine driver said; 'If you're not scared I guess I ain't.' Van Horne liked 'fat and bulgy' things like himself. He designed the sleeping car berths to match his girth. But he had a gentler side, collecting Japanese porcelain and French Impressionists, and played his violin in the stillness of the Rockies.

Above: Construction workers of the St Paul, Minneapolis & Manitoba Railway stand atop their dormitory cars. The military escort was to guard against hostile Indians.
Right: This historic SPM&M locomotive arrived by river barge in 1861 to run between St Paul and St Anthony.

Across the Prairies

'The so-called Prairie Section is not prairie at all in the sense that the Red River Valley is a prairie. The country west of Portage la Prairie is a broken rolling country . . . it is costing us a great deal more than the subsidy and a great deal more than we expected.'

George Stephen to Sir John A Macdonald, 1882

George Stephen remains a shadowy figure in Canadian history, especially in contrast to the flamboyant Van Horne. But they got on well together, and the American once said, 'Stephen did more work and harder work than I did . . . I only had to spend the money, but Stephen had to find it when nobody in the world believed [in the railway] but ourselves.'

The political hurdles had been overcome, although British, American and Canadian newspapers continued to snipe at the enterprise. On 1 September 1881, the British periodical *Truth* noted that the CPR had launched its bonds. The railway, it claimed, 'will run, if it is ever finished, through a country frost-bound for seven or eight months of the year . . .' British Columbia, dismissed as a 'barren, cold mountain country that is not worth keeping,' could not be 'galvanized into prosperity by fifty railroads.' *Truth* did not think that even New Yorkers were 'such fools as to put their money into this mad project.' Two years later, on 17 November 1883, the *Wall Street Daily News* called the railway a 'Northwest wildcat,' and its stock a 'dead skin.'

Stephen estimated the cost of the road at $45 million. To avoid fixed charges he refused to issue mortgage bonds. To the $25 million from the government, the Syndicate added $6.1 million from the sale of shares to directors and others. Stephen resigned from the Bank of Montreal in June 1881 to devote his full time to the CPR, and to avoid any conflict of interest, since the bank handled the land grant bonds. He held back on a public offering of shares until the CPR had some cash flow from sales of land, and from freight and passengers on the completed sections of the line. The more successful Van Horne was in laying track, the more money Stephen had to raise. Both knew that transcontinental – not local – traffic would generate the revenue they needed.

Van Horne promised to complete 500 miles of main line across the prairies by the end of 1882. He almost made it. In the spring the Red River flooded, cutting off the supply route between Winnipeg and the United States. Railway construction had created a corps of trained men who went home each winter. Van Horne drew them into his scheme, and hired men who had come west in search of new opportunities.

The track-laying, done entirely by hand, required an efficient supply system. Van Horne hired Thomas Shaughnessy, general storekeeper of his former company, in November 1882. Aged 29, Shaughnessy arrived in Winnipeg dressed like a dandy in black felt hat, black tie, morning coat and light striped trousers – and went immediately to work. The previous government attempts at railroad building had suffered because the friends of politicians quickly stuck their noses in the trough, demanding jobs and special deals in supplying the project. Shaughnessy, as general purchasing agent, soon showed that only 'price, quality and rapidity of delivery' mattered to him. No one, not even friends of directors, received special consideration. Shaughnessy also showed great skill in keeping creditors at bay when the line ran out of money.

In February 1882 a contract for the 675 miles from Oak Lake in western Manitoba to the end of the prairie section at the Bow River near Calgary was awarded to Shepard and Company of St Paul.

The work went astonishingly well. The railway route was located and staked by CPR surveyors and engineers. Then construction crews graded the line, prepared the roadbed, laid the ties and hammered home the spikes that held the rails

Above: The famed 'tracklaying machine' is shown in use, possibly on the Algoma Branch. Later it was used on the main line west of Sudbury.
Below: Flimsy, non-standard construction marked this timber trestle near the Lake of the Woods. When CPR took over the Lakehead-Winnipeg section in 1881-83, these were replaced with earth fills.

The way of life of the Plains tribes was altered forever by the building of the transcontinental railroads. The bones of buffalo (an animal once a major part of the Indian lifestyle) were used by white men as fertilizer. The bones are being loaded into a CPR boxcar near Moose Jaw, Saskatchewan, in the late 1880s.

in place. The grade stayed above ground level to keep it snow free. Construction depots at 100-mile intervals held material and supplies to be sorted and forwarded in train lots. Steel rails came from the Krupp works in Germany and from England, tamarack ties from the forests of the Lake of the Woods. Crews erected stations at eight-mile intervals. One group would frame the building, the next enclose it, and the third plaster and paint it. Four or five identical stations were built at one time, and no community could boast that it had a better one than its neighbour. Telegraph lines paralleled the railway, and soon the chatter of the Morse key joined the other prairie noises. Division points at 125-mile intervals allowed for crew and locomotive changes, and for refuelling.

Every town wanted a water tank — 'to make the place look busier,' one westerner claimed. The CPR's 'Flying Wing' followed the contractor's crews, to ensure that everything was up to the standards set by Van Horne.

Grading ended on 13 November when the frost came, but track-laying went on until the end of the year. By that time, the crews had built 419.86 miles of main line, 28 miles of sidings, and a 100-mile branch line in Manitoba. By early October, trains were running to Pile of Bones, on Wascana Creek, later to be known as Regina, capital of the Northwest Territories. Van Horne, an avid gardener, realized the value

On a perfect summer day Locomotive No 14 puffs across the vast prairie. This still is from the CBC documentary drama 'National Dream.'

of the buffalo bones that strewed the prairies. They had been left by the Indians to ensure the return of the great beasts. Van Horne paid the Indians, Métis and settlers $4.50 to $5 a ton to collect them and sold them in the east as fertilizer.

Early in 1883, Langdon and Shepherd, railway contractors, ran advertisements offering wages of $1.50 a day with board at $4.50 a week for 'good, able-bodied, steady men' to build the railway. They were asked to 'apply on the work at end of track, now near Cypress Hills, about 600 miles west of Winnipeg.' Track-laying began on 18 April 1883. On 48 consecutive working days — Sunday was the only day of rest — crews laid an average of 3.46 miles of track a day. On two days, they laid over six miles.

The railway brought in settlers who sought to buy land

cheaply. In Winnipeg, citizens held 'indignation meetings' to protest the high price for lots being charged by the Canada North West Land Company, the selling agent for government and CPR land. As the track approached Moose Jaw, James H Ross and three others homesteaded on a nearby bluff in January 1882. The others soon sold out, but Ross remained to become the largest landlord in the new community created by the railway. In the summer of 1882, the Company raised money by selling five million acres of its land in 47 townsites to the Canada North West land company at $2.70 an acre, for a total of $13.5 million. Controlling interest in the land company belonged to Donald Smith, British aristocrats, and eastern Canadian capitalists. They resold the land at $6 an acre, payable over six years at 6 percent interest. Land in the

Moose Jaw townsite went for $30 an acre – half the profits went to the CPR. At that time, the community consisted of frame buildings and tents. The wind blew through cracks in the walls of the first church, the post office was a packing crate near the station, and the stench from dead horses worked to death by contractors pervaded the town when the wind blew in the wrong direction.

Whores and gamblers flocked to the construction camps to alleviate the monotony of life there. The sale of liquor was forbidden in the Northwest Territories, and the Mounties strove valiantly to stamp out bootleggers, hampered by their number and ingenuity and their own need for strong drink to relieve the monotony of policing the plains. On 1 January 1883, Van Horne wrote to NWMP Commissioner Irvine: 'On no great work within my knowledge where so many men have been employed has such perfect order prevailed.'

The Indians gave little trouble, although they unnerved the crews by silently watching them at work. When the Cree chief Piapot and his people pitched their tents on the right of way in 1882, a Mountie pulled out his watch and gave them 15 minutes to move. When they refused, he kicked down the center pole of Piapot's tent, then did the same to the other lodges. Father Albert Lacombe, an Oblate missionary whom the Indians trusted, averted trouble when the track encroached on the Blackfoot reservation at Gleichen in July 1883. Later Van Horne entertained the chief and the priest in his private railway car, giving each a lifetime pass on the railway. One story claims that he also made Father Lacombe president of the line for an hour for his services. Like other CPR legends, this one grew with the telling. One version claims that the priest promptly ordered that all materials for his mission henceforth be carried free, and also issued himself two lifetime passes. Even if this incident did not happen, it illustrates how the CPR was viewed as it moved into the west. If it threatened traditional ways of life, it could also be the source of riches for those who knew how to manipulate it.

Turner Bone, a Scottish CPR engineer, recalled in later life how he travelled west on a freight train in 1883, on a car loaded with telegraph poles: 'I quite enjoyed the novelty of the ride.' He stumbled off the train at night to be met by a CPR night watchman who took him to the Royal Hotel, 'a large marquee tent.' At that time, the construction crews were 12 miles beyond Medicine Hat. In his eighties, Bone could 'still picture the busy scene, and . . . hear the clang of the rails as they were dropped on the ties.' End of track 'was something more than the point to which the track had been laid. It was a real live community, a hive of industry' in an empty land. In late June, the temperature soared to 107°F, then plunged to 58°F as a storm swept through the camp on 2 July. Everything blew down. Dry sand from the sidings filled the air, and ripped the tracings of plans from the work tables.

The rails reached Calgary on 13 August 1883.

By the time the Indians had ceased to be a menace and had become tourist attractions. Every visitor wanted to photograph them, but they would cover up their faces or demand money. Commissioner Irvine reported in 1883 that 'the Indians were so kept in subjection that no opposition of any moment [to the railway] was encountered from them.' Piapot had styled himself 'Lord of Heaven and Earth.' A photograph of him later in life shows him dressed in a blanket coat, cradling a rifle, baring his teeth in a half-grin, half-snarl. This picture was sold to tourists who had come to see the wonders of the railway and of the west. On the stock of the rifle appear the words: 'Pi-a-Pot copyrighted J A Brock, Brandon.'

Along Lake Superior

'Two hundred miles of engineering impossibility.'
William Cornelius Van Horne

Van Horne had no illusions about the difficulties of building the 650-mile line across the Laurentian Shield between Callander and Port Arthur. Hard old rocks thrust south to meet the waters of Lake Superior, offering no hope of settlement or of local traffic. This land, untraveled by whites, offered little to sustain life. Twisted rocks, numerous lakes, short, fast streams and thick forests strewn with windfalls made passage on foot difficult. Bitterly cold in winter, the land turned into a morass of swamp and muskeg in summer when the heat and the mosquitoes, no-see-ums and other pests tormented men and beasts.

The only advantage the stretch along Lake Superior offered was the possibility of supply by water. In 1883 the CPR bought the *Champion No. 2* – its first shipping venture.

Turner Bone noted that this wilderness did not deter George Middleton who surveyed the Lake Superior section for the CPR. He took only a brush and comb and an extra pair of socks in his pocket when he traveled: 'He told me that he made no written report on that survey, but had just gone to Van Horne and told him all about it.'

The line between Winnipeg and Port Arthur, built under government contract, had been completed on 17 June 1882. Poorly sited and badly ballasted, the tracks had begun to show wear and tear in the following year, with rails becoming bent and worn. Sidings, stations, freight sheds, yards and engine facilities had not been built. The Company took over the line in May 1883, and received just under $1 million from the government to bring it up to standard. The first scheduled passenger train between Port Arthur and Winnipeg ran on 10 June, and Van Horne began to negotiate for the construction of elevators at the head of the lake.

The shoddy work slowed down traffic, as the CPR upgraded the line. In September the track near Oxdrift sank into the ground, requiring piles to be driven 135 feet into the muck to support it. In November, a trestle collapsed under an eastbound grain train. Then an iron bridge failed. Forest fires burned down telegraph poles and consumed ties during that hot summer.

Van Horne marshalled 12,000 men, 5000 horses and 300 dog teams in 1883-1884 to build the section round Lake Superior. He tried to ensure that the men were well fed, but encountered problems in keeping the demon drink out of the

Above: A curving section of fill crosses Jack Fish Bay. This particularly difficult section of track, including a tunnel, cost $700,000 to build.

Below: A construction camp on Lake Superior's north shore lies just to the left of the route. The hard-working navvies have already cut down trees and cleared brush.

camps. The Ontario government, eager to cash in on the construction boom, issued liquor licenses to traders – but did not set up any system of controlling the resulting excesses.

John Macoun visited the north shore of Lake Superior with his son in the summer of 1884. 'Tormented by flies,' he walked towards a cutting just as the workmen set off an explosion. They retreated to a shanty, which Macoun did not reach in time. But 'no stones came near me,' he reported. Macoun found that the 'whisky pedlars were so bad that they had disorganized the whole work on the line.' At one camp, a half-drunken teamster objected to young Macoun's appearance. When Macoun reproved him, the man 'immediately pulled out a pistol and swore he would blow my brains out.' The naturalist had been appointed magistrate for the County of Hastings, but had no jurisdiction on the north shore. But 'being a good temperance advocate, I was easily pressed and swore in two special constables who immediately went to work and confiscated all the whisky in the camp and around it, and took the owners prisoners.'

It's easy to understand why men sought escape in drink. Railway construction created a new Canadian class, the 'bunkhouse men,' who lived in dank dwellings, slept on straw mattresses and ate salt pork, beans, molasses, potatoes, oatmeal, tea and bread. At times even these ran short because of poor organization and careless contractors. In May 1884, 300 men at one camp had only three-quarters of a barrel of flour, a week's supply of pork, and no sugar, beans or other foodstuffs.

Work proceeded slowly in 1883. By the end of the year, the end of track lay ten miles west of Sudbury.

In mid-March, 1884, Van Horne received a 'special informal report' from an inspecting engineer. 'Men are plentiful, but the supply of horses and plant is utterly inadequate to the work or "portaging" and grading,' it said. Nor were there enough dump cars, wheelbarrows, drills, picks and shovels. Van Horne induced James Worthington, who had built only 130 miles of new railway during the three years he had supervised construction, to retire. On 1 May 1884, Harry Abbott took charge of building the line west of Sudbury. After his first inspection trip, Abbott reported that he had found everything 'in worse condition than I had anticipated.' It took his train 4½ hours to cover 22 miles. Abbott increased the maintenance crews, doubled the work force building a trestle and checked the food supplies. He also found that 'liquor sellers are becoming troublesome.'

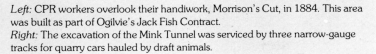

Left: CPR workers overlook their handiwork, Morrison's Cut, in 1884. This area was built as part of Ogilvie's Jack Fish Contract.
Right: The excavation of the Mink Tunnel was serviced by three narrow-gauge tracks for quarry cars hauled by draft animals.

The navvies began to encounter rock where soil had been expected as the line moved towards the Pic River where it drained into Lake Superior. In places, seemingly solid sections of the line collapsed under trains, and had to be rerouted. Elsewhere, these sink holes had to be filled with rock.

Money began to run short. John Ross, building the section east of Nipigon, used masonry where Van Horne believed that timber and fill would serve just as well. Trains could travel at slow speeds for two or three years until more solid structures could be built to replace any temporary works, he argued. Storm waters on Lake Superior licked away the rock banks constructed to support the line and other works. Tunnels had to be hacked through the granite where it lined the lakeshore. Dynamite cost $7.5 million, and three miles of track near Jack Fish, $1.2 million.

By mid-March 1885, only five gaps totalling 98 miles remained between Port Arthur and Sudbury.

But the cost of this 'national link' had strained the Company's resources, and almost pushed it into receivership. The CPR had spent $56,695,377 up to 31 December 1883, of which it had raised $37,377,151, the rest coming from government subsidies and land sales. The line generated some revenue, but its most costly sections along Lake Superior and through the western mountains drained its cash resources.

This steam shovel was built by the Bucyrus Steam Shovel Manufacturing Company of Bucyrus, Ohio. It is shown here working in a ballast pit.

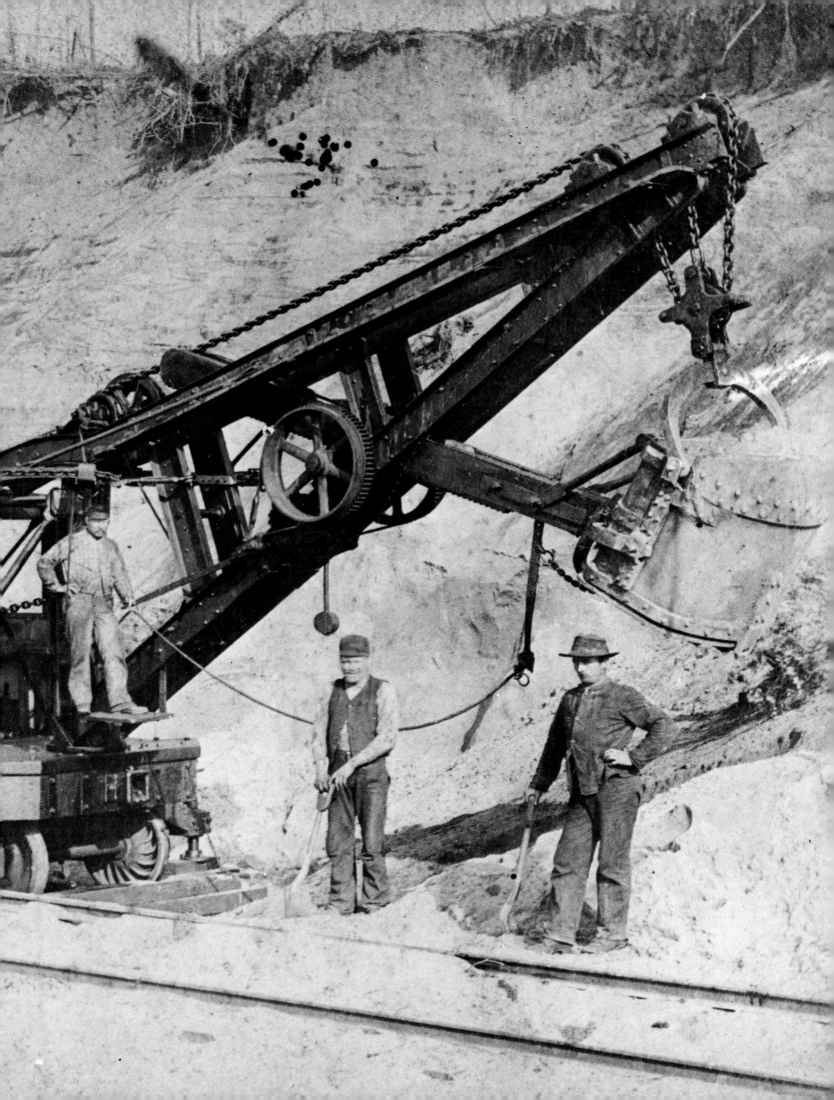

The western land boom collapsed in 1883, and a severe frost ravaged the prairie crops in September. Manitobans hated the CPR for its high freight rates and its monopoly. The market for railway securities had been damaged when the Northern Pacific went into receivership, and an economic depression still gripped Canada. Stephen needed hard cash to keep construction moving. Macdonald hoped that a government dividend guarantee for CPR stock would rescue the company.

Rather unwisely, Van Horne had told the *Montreal Star:* 'The CPR has never estimated the cost of any work. It has not had time for that . . . If we haven't got enough, we will get more, that's all about it.'

Liberal leader Edward Blake quoted these words in the House of Commons in February 1884 as the financial plight of the railway worsened. Macdonald introduced a railway relief bill that provided a $22.5 million loan to the railway, and it became law on 6 March. But Stephen had mortgaged the line to secure this money. On 19 July the Prime Minister informed him that he 'must not look for any more legislative assistance for the CPR', but rather 'work out your own salvation.' According to one story, John Henry Pope, acting Minister of Railways, told Macdonald: 'The day after the Canadian Pacific busts, the Conservative party busts the day after,' and this thought must have tortured the aging prime minister as the costs of the line escalated through 1884.

On 9 February 1885 Stephen wrote to Macdonald, pointing out that he and Donald Smith had endorsed a five months' note for $1 million to keep the Company operating, adding: 'I venture to say that what Smith and I have done and are doing individually, is simply absurd on any kind of business grounds. I venture to say that there is not a business man in all of Canada, knowing the facts, but would say we were a couple of fools for our pains.' Treasury officials had even made an inventory of Stephen's assets – including the china and household linen in his Montreal mansion – and Van Horne and senior staff took a 20 percent pay cut.

Macdonald, tired and beset by provinces demanding help for their railways, did not dare to try to convince his cabinet that just one more infusion of cash would save the CPR. In mid-March, Stephen proposed to the government that it turn

Above: A view of the newly-laid main line at Jack Fish Tunnel in the spring of 1885. The new tracks were unballasted, but troop trains, moving at 5 mph, passed here moving troops to suppress the Northwest Rebellion.
Above left: A newly-excavated rock cut north of Lake Superior.

its $35 million in unissued CPR shares into first mortgage bonds – and let the Company have $5 million immediately. The cabinet rejected the plan, and Stephen sent a sad little note to Macdonald lamenting the demise of their dream. On 17 March 1885, Sir John wrote to Charles Tupper: 'How it will end God knows – but I wish I were well out of it.'

But when Senator Frank Smith, an influential Conservative, championed Stephen's cause, the cabinet agreed to give the funding idea further consideration.

Then a western radical saved the capitalists.

On the day that Stephen wrote his note, the second Riel rebellion erupted – sparked in part by the arrival of the railway in the west and its impact on the lives of the Métis. Many of these people had moved west from Manitoba into

the Northwest Territories, settling on the North Saskatchewan River. The CPR destroyed their transportation system, the hated surveyors moved over the land, and a remote and incompetent bureaucracy delayed their acquisition of land.

This time, Riel had with him Gabriel Dumont, an able guerrilla leader. In March 1885 the rebels cut the telegraph wires at Batoche, their headquarters south of Prince Albert. A force of Mounties and militia sent to put down the rebellion suffered a defeat by Dumont at Duck Lake. The Indians attacked a mission and forced the Mounties to abandon Fort Pitt.

The federal government did not have enough troops in the west to suppress the rebellion. The Mounties formed a thin red line across the prairies, and a handful of them had to contain a strike in the Rockies on 1 April.

But Canada did have a railway line to the west.

Van Horne promised to move troops to Qu'appelle, the station nearest the uprising, in 11 days. He bent his organizing genius and the resources of the railway to this task. Troops marched or sleighed over the 89 mile gap in the line, travelling on flatcars where no coaches were available before speeding across the prairies.

The CPR saved itself by saving the west.

Even before the Riel Rebellion collapsed at the Battle of Batoche on 9 May, Macdonald had announced a bill to assist the CPR. The last of the missing links in the Lake Superior section was closed. Van Horne even organized a last spike ceremony on the shore of Jack Fish Bay on 16 May for Lieutenant Colonel Oswald, one of the commanders of the troops. The victorious soldiers returned home all the way by rail, singing the praises of the CPR.

The bill to aid the CPR cleared the House on 10 July.

On 16 November 1885, nine days after the final last spike was driven in the Rockies, Louis Riel died on the gallows in Regina. Van Horne claimed that 'in simple gratitude, the Company ought to erect a monument to Riel as its greatest benefactor.'

Through the Rockies

'Have no means of paying wages, pay car can't be sent out, and unless we get immediate relief we must stop. Please inform Premier and Finance Minister. Do not blame me if an immediate and most serious catastrophe happens.'
Van Horne to Donald Smith, 15 April 1885

Van Horne's wire to Smith indicates how taut nerves had become in the spring of 1885. Crews were working from west and east to complete the line through the western mountains. Andrew Onderdonk and his men drove in from Yale, the head of navigation of the Fraser River. The mountain section started at Calgary. From here James Ross, the CPR's manager of construction, pushed the track through the mountains towards the line moving from the coast.

A blast of dynamite at Yale on 14 May 1980 had made known the start of construction of the western part of the line.

Three mountain chains lie between tidewater and Calgary. A profile of the line drawn by the CPR in 1886 shows the long slope from the prairies into the Rockies, reaching a summit at 5296 feet. Then the profile plunges sharply below the Kicking Horse Pass to the valley of the Columbia River. The Selkirk Mountains, pierced by Rogers Pass at 4300 feet, appear as a single pyramid, and then the line drops steeply again to the Columbia Range and Eagle Pass at just under 2000 feet.

Sandford Fleming and his party barely averaged three miles a day on the survey through these mountains. Dripping rain from bushes and branches soaked them, devil's club clawed at them, fallen trees tripped them, and they had to cross patches of skunk cabbage – 'acres of stinking perfection.' And all around loomed the mountains, magnificent and menacing, cutting off the sun as the men stumbled through the valleys.

Fleming had selected the Yellowhead Pass through the Selkirks. But 'Hell's Bells' Rogers had located the more southerly pass named for him. It looked like a good idea at the time to take the line through Rogers Pass. A Scottish elder once remarked, 'The fact is that if the good Lord had not bored through the mountains with rivers, there is not enough money in the Empire to build to the coast.' This pious sense of certainty about the divine order kept men like Stephen and Van Horne going when the money ran out and the physical obstacles seemed unsurmountable.

The track followed some of the river valleys the Good Lord had provided. But the line had to be notched into the sheer face of canyon walls, pushed through rock, and carried on spider's web trestles across rivers. The grade had to be kept at 2.2 percent, a drop or rise of 116 feet in a mile.

Andrew Onderdonk, under the government contract, used a mixed force of Chinese, Americans and Canadians to carve the line through the coastal mountains. From Yale the line followed the west bank of the Fraser River, crossed it, then headed inland along the Thompson. Onderdonk used the Caribou Road to supply the line, and took his sternwheeler *Skuzzy* through Hell Gate for use on the Upper Fraser and Thompson. One hundred and fifty of 'Onderdonk's Lambs' – the Chinese workers – hauled the vessel upriver against the current. The Chinese had been employed in railroad construction in the United States, and came to Canada from there and in batches from China as contract labourers. Earning a pittance, living on rice and salmon, meticulously clean, they dreamed of a return home or of a new life in the 'gold mountain.' The Chinese did most of the heavy rock work, while the whites did the easier timber work, cutting trees and building trestles. The workers carved fifteen tunnels along the lower Fraser. In February 1882 Onderdonk turned his crews around and began the line between Yale and Port Moody at tidewater. The last spike on this section was driven on 22 January 1884.

The local press blew hot and cold about the new railroad – an indicator of the ambivalence that Canadians would develop towards this new national institution. While complaining that the $5.50 fare between Port Moody and Yale was thrice that for the same distance in England, the *Port Moody Gazette* also wrote about the 'iron horse' bounding over the Fraser and taking Lytton by storm.

By the end of 1884, Onderdonk's men had pushed the line to Savona, heading towards the old Hudson's Bay Company post at Kamloops, and the lakes in the shadow of the Selkirks. The government-built section of the line had a rickety look to it. A tunnel through a mud cliff collapsed, so the line was run around it on trestles. The *Port Moody Gazette* complained on

Right: Onderdonk's crews work in the forested lower Fraser Valley in 1883. The railroad ties, piled on flatcars, are being unloaded and carried forward on the shoulders of the tracklayers.

Above: On the original transcontinental railway there was no structure
which surpassed the Mountain Creek Bridge in the Selkirks. Constructed of more
than two million board feet of timber, it was 164 feet high and 1086 feet long. In its
own way it was a thing of beauty.
Left: Another view of the towering bridge; Locomotive No 132 pauses with its cars
extending back past mid-span. Another locomotive can be seen to the right at the far
end of the bridge.

6 September that 'along the line you will see signs of the
stupidity and want of engineering skill that are always visible
on railroads where death comes without warning.' Van
Horne, himself bent on cutting every corner to conserve the
CPR's scarce funds, described the truss bridges on this
section as the 'worst I ever saw in a railway.'

The CPR crews building the line from Calgary through the
Rockies had a sense of high adventure about the project.
Turner Bone had travelled to the tent town of Calgary in
1883 on a train which had 'rolled and pitched like a ship in a
choppy sea.' He laid out and superintended the construction
of a round house and a turntable, then encountered the
power of the conductor and the emerging bureaucratization
of the CPR. He'd put his stuff on a flatcar, but the train did not
move. The conductor was 'waiting for orders,' the usual
answer 'given by the conductor of a construction train which
might be waiting – for no apparent reason – at a siding when
anyone ventured the remark: "What are we waiting for?" '

The Indians thought the 'crazy white men' were driving
stakes in the ground to find their way back – and played a
trick on them by pulling them up.

One of these crazy white men in Bone's crew started to
drag a survey chain across a frozen lake. The ice gave way,
but he ploughed on and smashed his way to the opposite
shore. The five men engineering crews received 125 pounds
of bacon, 65 pounds of ham and 30 pounds of oatmeal and
other food to last them a month. Itinerant photographers
wandered along the line, and two clergymen ministered to
the spiritual needs of the men. Bone mentions a contractor
named Isaacs, a hotel owner from Niagara Falls with no
experience in railway building. He ran a popular camp –
'everything had to be neat and tidy. No rubbish lying
around.'

Men constantly arrived to work on the road. Bob Woods,
known as Dago Driver, 'marshalled them at HQ' and took
them out to the camps. He was 'like a general in command of
an army, riding along the tote road with his company.' Bone
relished the life in the mountains. He missed the 'rhythmic
sound of the tumbling waters of the Kicking Horse River'
when his camp moved to Golden, and had difficulty sleeping

Workers halt their labors on a timber retaining wall near Eleven Shed in Rogers Pass. Note that this is the era before specially-designed work clothes, and the workers wear old conventional clothing. Due to a prevalent fear of sunstroke, all the men are wearing hats.

Above: A cut was made through the nose of Sailor Bar Bluff, 7 miles above Yale. The navvies are dwarfed by this huge rock outcropping.

Left: This photograph shows one of six tunnels that were to be constructed in the Cherry Creek bluffs. The south shore of Kamloops Lake was a region of deep coves which were marked by these rocky buttresses.

Left inset: A pile-driver operated by Onderdonk's men is at work on the trestle over the Nocola River in 1884. In the background can be seen the barren hills of the upper Thompson Valley.

near the quiet waters of the Columbia. At Christmas, 1884, the crew, which had become 'just like members of one large family,' ended their party with a shout of 'Hurrah for the CPR.'

Bone, an engineer who had walked the three miles back and forth to school at the age of seven, typified the hardy men who saw in the building of the CPR the moral equivalent of war. Taking the line through the mountains set man against nature in a titanic struggle. The Reverend R G MacBeth knew many of the railway men and claims that these contractors 'did not, by any means, always make money. But . . . very few of the contractors or engineers cared for the money end of it in any case. They felt that they were engaged in a work of

Left: Eagle Pass, British Columbia, on 7 November 1885, about 9:20 am. Honorable Donald A Smith, later Lord Strathcona and Mount Royal, faces the camera as he prepares to drive the ordinary iron spike completing the Canadian Pacific Railway transcontinental main line between the Atlantic and the Pacific Oceans.
Below: Donald A Smith drives home the last spike. To his left is Stanford Fleming (white beard and top hat). To his right stands William C Van Horne (black beard and bowler hat). Just out of sight to the left stands Major Rogers: his Scottish hat rests on the tie to the left of the spike. The youth behind Smith is Edward Mallandaine.

significance, not only to Canada and the Empire, but to the world, and that was an inspiration worth while.'

Those like Bone who were employed by the CPR enjoyed the benefits of being skilled specialists in a large, dynamic company. The contracted labour had a much tougher time, and these largely illiterate men left few records of their life on the line. Melchior Eberts fell to his death above Kamloops Lake in 1881. But most of those who died building the line remain nameless. Such men were buried in the mountains under a cross bearing the words 'Died on the Railroad.'

Morley Roberts, a man of education, wrote a song: 'Some of us are bums, some of us are farmers.' But all, he claimed, were 'jolly fellows.' The crews drilled, blasted, broke up stones and smoothed the way for the coming of the rails. In the mountains, they worked on three benches, the safest being at the top where no stones and other debris showered down from above. Day began with breakfast, then the foreman shouted 'Hook up!' The men worked for five hours before 'unhooking' for dinner and then put in another five hours work, often in rain and mud in a gloomy river valley. The contractors and the bosses lived above the huddle of tents and shacks that housed the labourers.

MacBeth caught the essence of the work when he wrote: 'In the grey half light of early morning . . . but little imagination would have been needed to believe that dimly-seen forms which peopled the rocky river banks were the advance guard of an army making its laborious way towards some naturally fortified stronghold.'

Sam Steele, in charge of the Mounties on the CPR line in the mountains, had a less romantic view of the work. With a few men he had to protect the work crews from the gamblers and the crooks who arrived at the camps to fleece the unwary. Forbidding the sale of liquor for ten miles on each side of the line did not prevent the flow of booze to the crews. The Mounties had also to intercede on behalf of the men when sub-contractors did not pay their wages. On 1 April 1885, when the CPR ran out of money and the navvies struck, Steele pleaded with their leaders to be patient. As Turner Bone put it: 'It was not a strike in the ordinary meaning of that word.' The money was needed to support homesteads in Manitoba, Minnesota and Dakota. When the strikers tried to stop tracklaying, Steele rose from his sick bed and threatened to fire on the mob approaching his police post. But he also brought the workers' plight to the attention of the government.

The line reached the British Columbia border on 25 May 1884, and the first station beyond it was named Stephen. By July, a tote road reached the Columbia at Golden, and grading was well under way along the difficult stretch of line bordering the Kicking Horse River which dropped steeply down towards the Columbia. Between Hector and Field, seven miles apart in a direct line, the road descended 1141 feet. The gradient of the track down the 'Big Hill' exceeded 4 percent, but Van Horne explained this was only a 'temporary measure.' Uphill spur lines on to which trains could be run to slow them down were built. Four locomotives hauled short freight trains uphill during the first years of operation. Westbound freights arrived with smoking wheels as engineers clamped on the brakes to slow their descent.

The Selkirks trapped the moisture laden clouds as they moved east, blanketing the slopes with snow. Avalanches and snow slides roared down the mountains at speeds as high as 200 mph. James Ross wrote to Van Horne on 19 February 1885: 'The men are frightened. I find the snowslides on the

Above: Revelstoke, British Columbia, was reached by the CPR through the tireless efforts of many men.
Left: A ballast train pulled by a former Virginia & Truckee locomotive approaches the south portal of Tunnel No 4, two miles above Yale. This is a typical steep-sided river valley of glacial origin.

Selkirks are much more serious than I anticipated, and I think are quite beyond your ideas of their magnitude and danger to the line.' Seven men had been buried under slides, and two had died.

Ross built the line beyond Rogers Pass to avoid the avalanche slopes and steep grades, using a series of trestles to create 'The Loop.' A peak named after him broods over this part of the line. Then Ross took the line through Eagle Pass in the Columbia (or Monashee) Mountains, and met Onderdonk's men coming from the west.

The final last spike was driven on 7 November 1885 at Craigellachie.

In Canada's most famous photograph, Donald Smith taps the spike home at 9:22 am Pacific time. Sandford Fleming, with a square white beard, stares four square into the camera. He had invented Standard Time after missing a train in Ireland, and this method of marking the hours would prove invaluable in running the railway of which he had been so much a part. Van Horne, hands in pocket, stomach well out front, looks on benignly. The last spike, he had said, would be 'just as good an iron one as there is between Montreal and Vancouver and anyone who wants to see it driven will have to pay full fare.'

As Smith bends to hit the spike – he bent it on the first try – a confident 17-year-old casually cocks his head behind him. That boy, Edward Mallandaine, had wanted to fight Indians.

Instead, he had gone into business for himself, running a freighting service to supply the railway. Mallandaine died in Creston, BC, in 1951. The triumph of the last spike that linked Canada together seems almost near enough to touch at times.

After it was driven, the cry went up: 'All aboard for the Pacific!' Sam Steele attended the ceremony, then rode from Kamloops to the sea in Onderdonk's private car. The train raced through tunnels at 57 mph, 'our short car whirling around the sharp curves like the tail of a kite.' By the time dinner was served, Steele was one of only three people unafflicted by 'train sickness.' He wrote: 'I think this was one of the wildest rides by rail that any of us had taken, and was, to say the least of it, dangerous.' On the following day, a train rushed out of the tunnel towards a trestle on which stood a handcart loaded with section hands. They jumped off, clung to the edge of the bridge, and watched the train smash their cart into the river below.

Turner Bone did not see the last spike driven. He and his crew packed up, and got ready to leave on a work train. It chugged down the line towards them – and passed the group without stopping.

The excitement and the enthusiasm of the construction phase – and the sheer, hard, backbreaking work and worry that had gone into it – had become part of Canada's history and image. The act that brought the CPR into being stated: 'And the Company shall thereafter and for ever efficiently maintain, work and run the Canadian Pacific Railway.'

Now the Company began to grow into a national force almost as strong as government and to rouse in Canadians that sense of ambiguity about its activities that persists to this day.

Spreading the Net:

1885-1896

'The CPR, though it had connected with the Pacific Ocean, was like a poor man with a large and growing family, who finds his boys pushing their legs through their breeches faster than he can conveniently cover them . . .'

David Hanna, *Trains of Recollection*, 1926

A lthough Van Horne claimed during the last spike cere- mony that 'the work [had] been done well in every way' the railway had many rickety and dangerous places.

One earlier traveller reported that his train has been stopped by a blizzard. He had been put in a common coach, although he had sleeping car tickets. At Banff the only food available was cheese and crackers. Rocks came through the windows and forest fires licked at the coaches as they passed through the Rockies. In the winter of 1885-1886, avalanches roared down the mountain slopes, closing the line. And the winter snows proved to be a major problem over the years, despite the work of men stationed in the mountains charged with ensuring that the trains got through on time.

When Van Horne took over as chairman and president in 1888, he set about making the line a first class trans- continental railway, building feeder lines, upgrading the track, and ordering locomotives and rolling stock. He also established the CPR style of management, combining efficiency and frugality during a period of economic recession.

Within a year of the last spike being driven, the CPR had cleared its debt with the government. The Syndicate also gained control of the Canada Central Railway, extended it to Ottawa and Callander, and ran its tracks into Toronto and Montreal. Between 1885 and 1890, the CPR moved into the Maritimes, assembling and building the 'Short Line' from Montreal through Maine to tidewater at Saint John. Windsor, Detroit, Duluth and St Paul were tied into the expanding network. Short eastern Canadian lines that made no economic sense – or money – became part of a national system that turned a profit. Out west, 'the CPR had every- thing . . . and, as a natural process . . . gobbled everything in the way of feeders and rivals . . .' as David Hanna put it. But, he added, 'every sane Canadian is proud of the CPR.'

This pride found expression in the reception the first trans- continental train received as it travelled across Canada. The

The original station at Port Arthur, Ontario in 1884 or 1885, constructed of unfinished pine. Well-dressed townspeople wait for the train to pull in. Others, perhaps having nothing better to do, pass the time of day.

special poster that trumpeted the departure shouted in red
'Our Own Line.' In smaller print, at the bottom of the poster,
were spelled out the benefits of the new line – 'No Customs,'
'No Delays,' 'No Transfers.'

Promptly at 8 pm on 28 June 1886, as the Montreal
Garrison Artillery fired a salute, the *Pacific Express* eased out
of the station. A fractured coupler delayed its departure from
Ottawa by two hours. At Carleton Place the express connected with the train from Toronto which had departed that
city without a demonstration.

Residents turned out in full force at stations along the line
and were allowed to inspect the luxurious diners and
sleepers. From its beginnings, the CPR sought to create an
aura of luxury and comfort, touched with a hint of imperial
grandeur and exoticism, around its passenger cars. Dining
cars carried the names of British royal palaces, sleeping cars
those of remote and romantic cities like Honolulu and
Yokohama. No expense was spared to maintain this aura:
The silver service in *Holyrood* cost $3000.

At Sudbury Junction some well-dressed, good-looking
girls greeted the train; evergreens and inscriptions such as
Vive La Confédération decorated the station. At Winnipeg,
the train received a salvo of artillery. The city now had a
population of 20,238, but much of the nearby prairie re-

Right: A CPR water tower is pictured near Fife, British Columbia.

mained empty and unsettled because of marshes and the activities of speculators. The train sped through green pastures and wheat fields to Brandon, with its population of 2348. The railway had created this town. Many of the lonely stations on the prairies would become the nuclei of new communities, dependent on the railway for their lives. The locomotive had to be replaced just beyond Broadview, so passengers strolled on the prairie, organized foot races and picked wild flowers – 'a jolly break in our ride across the plains,' as one passenger put it.

At the station named after him, passengers met Crowfoot. They presented him with a speech, passed the hat, and handed him a few dollars 'for the trouble he had taken in accepting our invitation' and went on their way through the Rockies. These mountains impressed and overawed the first travellers as they would all future ones. The train passed gangs of Chinese: At one camp, their cook took one look at the passengers and then went on preparing a meal. The people of Victoria came to Port Moody to greet the train on its arrival there on 4 July. It had taken 139 hours to travel 2892.6 miles – and arrived on time.

The second *Atlantic Express,* which left Port Moody on 7 July, passed through blazing forests and valleys down which strong winds blew during an exceptionally hot summer. Derailed by a toppling wood pile, the cars caught fire. This disaster, and other minor derailments and collisions, did little to dampen the enthusiasm of early train travellers. And they helped to build an *esprit de corps* among railroaders as they learned to work together as part of a vast national system. The west had begun to wake up. By 1886, 163,000 people lived in Manitoba and the North-West Territories. Despite poor economic conditions, a sense of excitement suffused the air and the new railway enhanced it, heightening feelings of national unity and of a shared destiny.

Below: This picture was taken on the occasion of the arrival of the first Canadian train from the Atlantic to the Pacific at Port Arthur, Ontario, 30 June 1886.

Above right: A typical small town scene with octagonal water tower and station building. This is East Coulee, Alberta, as photographed by Stan Stiles in June 1969.

Sir John A Macdonald left Ottawa on a special train on 9 July. He'd expected to be looking down on his railway 'from another sphere,' he said, adding: 'My friends in the Opposition kindly suggested that I would more likely be looking up from below.' He had, however, 'seen both friends and foes travelling over the road.' Lady Agnes Macdonald had already become an enthusiastic supporter of the railway after travelling on the uncompleted line to the Rockies in late 1885. She had been thrilled by 'the most interesting and delightful trip I ever made in my life.' She caught the enthusiasm of an age when she wrote to a friend:

What astonished me was the comfort and ease of the railway, its strict punctuality, its quiet and prompt management and its little motion. We read, played cards, wrote letters, all generally with great ease and this on a line far away in an almost uninhabited country and in the depths of a Canadian winter.

She also noted the contrast between the two Canadas that the railway now joined together:

Ottawa seems so dull and tame and stupid and *old* after that new wonderful western world with its breadth and length and clear air and wonderfully exhilerating atmosphere that always seems to lure me on.

The title of a book published in 1872, *The Great Lone Land,* caught the essence of the west at that time. In 1886, the *Lethbridge News* reported that an American had referred to this region as 'God's Country.'

The remarkable Lady Macdonald wanted her fill of this new land, and chose an unusual way to see it. She sat on a box secured to the cow catcher when she travelled west with her husband in 1886. Through Kicking Horse Pass, down the Big Hill, across Rogers Pass and on to Port Moody she went. 'Every possible sense of fear is lost in wonder and delight,' she wrote in an article in *Murray's Magazine.* Spring water sprayed the train in a 'wet' tunnel, so Lady Macdonald doffed her bonnet and put up an umbrella. Then she rode, unafraid, through the Fraser valley, 'black with wild rugged rocks, and awful with immense shadows.'

Lady Macdonald provided Van Horne with the sort of publicity for the line that money could not buy. In 1882, the CPR had net earnings of about $400,000. By 1885, these had risen to almost $2.4 million. Railway mileage expanded from 3998 miles in 1885 to 6476 in 1896, and the line was continually improved and well maintained. In 1890, over 200 wooden bridges were replaced by permanent structures, and an equal number built in 1891. A photograph from 1894 shows a section hand setting out on an inspection trip in a boat after heavy rains flooded the track.

The Company made money any and every way it could.

Van Horne had a vision of Vancouver in 1884 as 'a great city there with steel tracks carrying endless trains of freight and passengers, an all-year port with fleets of vessels trading with the world.' The Company received 6000 acres in government land grants in 1885; its townsite covered much of what is now the city's central business district. A plaque at the corner of Hastings and Hamilton streets in downtown Vancouver states: 'Here stood Hamilton. First Land Commissioner. Canadian Pacific Railway. 1885. In the silent solitude of the primeval forest. He drove a wooden stake in the earth and commenced to measure an empty land into the streets of Vancouver.' When Turner Bone visited the townsite in the following year he saw only 'burned stumps.' A careless CPR slash clearing crew set fire to the primeval forest, and destroyed the infant settlement and the older townsite of Granville.

The first transcontinental train reached Vancouver on 23 May 1887, decked out with a picture of Queen Victoria on the smokestack. At that time, the city had a population of only 2000, but by the following year the Company had made $868,000 from land sales in the new community.

In 1886, trains began to cross Canada with tea from China and Japan. Then came the silk trains that delivered silk from Japan to New York in 13 days. These once-famous trains, dull-painted and windowless, had priority over all others, and flashed from Vancouver to Montreal in 80 hours. When the prairies yielded a bumper harvest in 1891 and labour became scarce, the CPR advertised for workers, offering transportation from any station in Ontario to the west for $15, and harvest specials began to run in July.

To westerners, and especially to Manitobans who had an elected government, the new railway proved to be a mixed blessing. In his 1923 *History of the Canadian Pacific Railway,* Harold Innis wrote that the completion of the main line was a 'significant landmark in the spread of civilization throughout Canada.' But, he added, 'western Canada has paid for the development of Canadian nationality.' The Manitoba legislature passed several bills to give charters to other railways to build lines, only to see them disallowed by the federal government. Thus were they constantly reminded of the power of the CPR and of their own lack of control over their own destiny. In the east, competition kept freight rates reasonable. But the CPR seemed bent on making every cent it could from its operations, and the monopoly clause in the government contract caused endless discontent among westerners. In vain did the Company plead that it had recognized a 'moral obligation' and spent $6.7 million on branch lines south of Winnipeg. By the end of 1887, George Stephen had become the most unpopular man in the west, with Van Horne running a close second. But Van Horne calmly noted that when Winnipegers burned Sir George in effigy, one mattress sufficed while it required two to do him justice.

Under political pressure, the federal government cancelled the Company's monopoly clause on 18 April 1888. But it guaranteed payment of interest on a new CPR bond issue of up to $15 million. In the fall of that year, another company built a line between Winnipeg and the border and then had the temerity to build a feeder line across the CPR track. The 'Battle of Fort Whyte' ensued as CPR crews ripped up the crossing and were confronted by the government's special constables and militia. A standoff ended with the replacement of the crossing, but the Company tended to treat any threat of competition as *lese-majesté* rather than as an attempt to serve the travelling public through better service and lower rates.

Van Horne, knighted in 1894, set the tone of the CPR when he upbraided a trainman who had argued with an irritable and unreasonable passenger:

You are not to consider your own feelings when you are dealing with these people. You should not have any. You are the road's while you are on duty; your reply is the road's: and the road's first law is courtesy.

Thirty-one snowsheds were built between Bear Creek and Ross Peak sidings. This view shows the complex structure of timbers which was necessary to protect the tracks from the enormous snowdrifts. Without snowsheds, winter passage would have been impossible. The project, begun in 1886, took two seasons to complete.

The Golden Years:

1897-1918

'We are not paupers. We can build the Crows Nest line without Governmental assistance if we see fit. But in view of what the Company has tried to do towards building up the interests of this country it is disappointing, to say the least, to be treated as a public enemy or a public menace.'

William Cornelius Van Horne, 1897

In 1893, a financial panic swept Canada. In that year, Van Horne wrote to his solicitor: 'The present times are the worst I have ever experienced, and I can see no sign of the better.' During the early 1890s, incomes and the price of wheat and other commodities on the prairies remained low.

But the railway continued to pay dividends. And it expanded its network. As mines opened in southeastern British Columbia, the CPR saw the danger of their output moving south of the border. James Hill built his Kaslo and Slocan line to carry ores to Kootenay Lake. From there, steamers took them to Bonner's Ferry, Idaho, the railhead of Hill's Great Northern Railway. The CPR leased and completed a 37-mile line, the Naksup and Slocan Railway, in 1894, to serve the mines in the Kootenay. The Company built a station and freight shed at Sandon. On 16 December, 1895, a special 'K & S' train drew into Sandon, carrying men hired by James Hill. They levelled the new freight shed, wrecked a trestle, pulled down the station and dumped it into a nearby creek.

The CPR had considered linking southeastern British Columbia with Fort Macleod to the east in 1889. In 1896, Laurier's Liberals came to power, and soon realized how vital to the nation's economy, especially in the west, the Company had become. Clifford Sifton, the Manitoban Minister of the Interior, believed that a railway from the Kootenay to the prairies had to be built to make 'every miner in British Columbia . . . a customer of the merchants of Winnipeg, Toronto and Montreal. Then we shall have taken one major step towards securing Canada for the Canadians.'

The CPR received a subsidy of $11,000 a mile to build the 182-mile line from Lethbridge to Kootenay Lake. It also agreed to cut its freight rates on the prairies. The Crowsnest Pass Agreement, passed on 29 June 1897, initially worked no hardship on the Company. When the rates bit into profits after the First World War, the CPR tried to raise them, with little success. For western farmers considered the 'Crow Rate' as unchangeable as the mountains through which the new line ran. The 1899 rates for grain, one half cent per ton mile,

Above: Between trains at the CPR station at Ottawa, Ontario in 1899. The pace slows down briefly near midday. Cabs await their next fare. Note the two shop girls taking a break by the side door.

Below: A grimy locomotive No 931, a 4-6-0, takes a breather near Brandon. Five hundred and two of these workhorse engines served with CPR and remained on the roster until 1960, the end of the steam era.

Below: Colonist sleeping cars are stopped in the Glacier House station, British Columbia. Snowsheds can be seen in the distance.
Right: CPR locomotives No 5760 and 5920 puff through the wooded hills and mountains east of Golden, British Columbia.

Above: Lord Shaughnessey was CPR's president and chairman of the board.
Far right: The Ten-Wheeler type 4-6-0 has to be the 'typical' CPR steam locomotive. Also called 'D-10,' built between 1905 and 1915, these sturdy, reliable engines formed the backbone of the CPR freight locomotive fleet.
Below: The CPR station at Lethbridge, Alberta, was quiet on a day in 1899. Note that the hand car at left appears to be loaded with baggage.

still held in 1982. The railways' loss in 1981-82 came to $641.1 million because of the 'Crow Rate.'

The exploitation of the workers who built the railway through the Crowsnest Pass led to a House of Commons enquiry. One man earned $387 for a year's work – and kept only $5.10 after contractors deducted expenses. Wages were fixed in camps, and men forbidden to leave – or even to talk at work in some places.

The depression began to lift in late 1896. In the following year, the Company's land sales doubled. George Stephen had recognized that a railway needed a populated west. As early as 1881, the Company stationed a land agent in London, and located a Land Commissioner in Winnipeg. A letter by Stephen in the London *Times* of 1 March 1883, suggested settling 10,000 Irish farmers in the northwest. In that year 100,000 immigrants had moved into the west, but no flood of newcomers followed the completion of the line. Droughts, early frosts, floods, grasshoppers and Riel scared them away. And there was plenty of free land left south of the border. Through the 1880s and early 1890s, a few people trickled into the Canadian west from Eastern Canada and the United States. In 1892, William Saunders developed Marquis Wheat, greatly extending the range of grain growing and the 'last best west' began to boom.

Van Horne told shareholders in 1898 that 'practically no mistakes have been made in the development of the system as far as we have gone.' He retired as president in the next year, handing over to Thomas Shaughnessy, a quiet man who expanded the CPR as Canada's economy boomed. In 1893, James Hill had completed the Great Northern, and the CPR had competition for freight. But the Company's land

policy began to pay off, and the CPR had the whole west to itself. CPR land went for $2.50 an acre, with a rebate of half of this if it came under cultivation in three to four years. The Company set up model farms, sent settlers back to their homelands to tell of the bounty and promise of the west, and toured display cars filled with crops around the country. In 1904, a large-scale irrigation scheme covering 220,000 acres began near Calgary. Wheat acreage almost tripled between 1905 and 1915. The railway also pioneered the use of film to promote development and issued pamphlets about the west in 40 languages. The federal government also launched a massive advertising campaign during these golden years, and it may be that many people say the Company as an agent of the government – or *vice versa*.

The railway provided steady income for immigrants as they struggled to establish themselves, and helped them to identify with their new country. D E MacIntyre, a Montrealer, supervised a gang of 30 Doukhobors in 1904 as they worked in a foot or two of cold water, straightening old rails and trimming them so that they could be relaid on branch lines and sidings. MacIntyre wrote:

> Every morning at about 10 o'clock, the CPR's crack passenger train, No. 1, appeared in the far distance. Standing on a rail pile [the Doukhobors] watched as it grew larger and larger. Then, when it was directly opposite us, it gave a long blow on its bull-throated whistle and the Douks as one man would stop and say 'Number One,' which was about all the English they knew.

The CPR strove valiantly to be all things to all people during the golden years between the end of the century and the close of the First World War. MacIntyre recalls the Company erecting tents and supplying cooking and sanitary facilities to immigrants stranded at a washed-out bridge in Saskatchewan. A burning trestle halted a train on Lake Superior. Some stubborn people refused to walk across the gap, claiming they'd paid to ride. Railroaders carried them over to the waiting train.

Other workers were less enchanted with the CPR, claiming that it paid low wages for long hours and operated in a feudal manner. The 'running trades' – engineers, conductors, firemen and trainmen, the aristocracy of the line – had a separate union which concentrated on gaining insurance and other benefits. The 'non-operating employees' made up the bulk of the labour force, caring for the track, the rolling stock, the stations and the passengers. At first, separate unions among these groups of workers came into being. In 1901, the Brotherhood of Maintenance of Way Employees organized a nationwide walkout and succeeded in raising their daily rate for a ten hour day from $1.25 to $1.50. Unions won minor concessions from the Company whose managers often fired those who joined them.

In November 1908 the Canadian Brotherhood of Railway Employees came into being in Moncton, and tried to obtain an agreement with the CPR. As the union's official history puts it: 'The Canadian Pacific management, from the very start, adopted a bitterly hostile attitude towards the Brotherhood.' They wanted only a union they could control. The Company fired members of the new union, and debarred clerical staff from joining it, 'because confidential records and reports might become public property.' A 1910 strike by CPR machinists for better working conditions failed. But on 4

Below: Joseph W Heckman took this photograph of the old wooden station at Sudbury Junction, Ontario around 1900. Note that the 'Sudbury Jct' sign above the Dominion Express Co door gives the distances to Montreal and Vancouver.
Right: The Sudbury station in 1915 was made of stone, replacing the previous wooden building.

November 1912, the Brotherhood organized a walkout as the grain traffic reached a peak. The strike forced the federal Minister of Labour to set up a board of conciliation so that disputes between workers and managers could be referred to a third party. The union called off the strike in January 1913.

Unionization disturbed the growth of the Company very little as it strode to greatness. The CPR had realized an Imperial dream – 'the all-red route to the Orient' – with its ships on the Pacific. In 1899 the crack new *Imperial Limited* linked Montreal and Vancouver in 100 hours. Luxurious hotels contributed to Company profits. The Scottish-baronial style of buildings favoured for the Chateau Frontenac in Quebec City, the Empress Hotel in Victoria and 'Windsor Castle,' the railway headquarters in Montreal, projected a solid image that hinted of noble origins.

An enterprising American decided to share the railway's wealth. Bill Miner stopped a CPR train near Mission, BC, on

10 September 1904, stole $7000 and lived quietly in nearby Princeton for two years, well liked by all. In 1906 he held up another train with the help of two companions, but found only $15 and a bottle of liver pills in the safe. This time he was caught, and the Grey Fox went to the British Columbia penitentiary but escaped over the border in 1907.

An anecdote from 1908 illustrates the style of the CPR. Charles Gordon, secretary to Thomas Shaughnessy, stuck a two cent stamp on an envelope, made an error, and threw the envelope away. Donald Smith came into the office, saw the envelope, retrieved it, and lifted off the unused two cent stamp. He slapped it down in front of Gordon, saying, 'That's not how we built the CPR.'

In 1882, the line had carried 388,785 passengers. By 1890, this number had risen to 2,685,730. In 1899, the CPR logged 1.373 *billion* passenger miles. Many passengers were tourists from Britain and the United States, come to see the wonders of the railway and the Rockies. Van Horne quickly grasped the tourist potential of his railway. The mountains that had made life so miserable for surveyors and construction crews became objects of romantic admiration when seen through the windows of one of the CPR's first class cars.

Left: This Joseph W Heckman photograph shows the CPR station at Winnipeg, Manitoba in August, 1899 as seen from the west.
Below: This Pacific type 4-6-2 was photographed at Calgary, Alberta in July 1946. The type was first produced after the turn of the century for use in New Zealand.

This view of the old and new stations in Québec City, Québec, taken in 1916, shows a contrast in size and architectural style.

68

'Since we can't export the scenery,' said Van Horne as he began to market the landscape, 'we'll import the tourists.'

Macdonald had stopped at the hot springs at Banff on his way home in 1886, and became a wilderness enthusiast. In June 1887 Parliament passed an act creating the 260-square-mile Rocky Mountain park to preserve the hot springs and the surrounding area.

Van Horne went on a promotional binge, designing some unusual advertising slogans to attract the right kind of tourists. 'How High We Live,' said the Duke to the Prince, 'on the Canadian Pacific Railway' linked aristocracy, good living and the Company. The first CPR pamphlet, issued in 1886, reproduced an article by the Marquis of Lorne, the former Governor-General. It claimed: 'Nowhere can finer scenery be enjoyed from the window of a car than upon this line.' The CPR built a hotel in Banff that stands out in the Bow Valley like a miniature mountain range, erected other hotels that resembled Swiss chalets, and imported guides to match, invited Edward Whymper, the famous mountaineer, to Canada, and issued a pamphlet on fishing and shooting that went into 30 editions. When the Bow River washed out the track in June 1894, local guide Tom Wilson suggested that the stranded passengers be entertained by the Indians. Thus began the annual Banff Indian days.

With wheat being exported by the railway from the prairies and tourists being imported into the Rockies, the CPR generated large profits. Net earnings rose from $12,230,165.49 in 1899 to $46,245,740.15 in 1913.

An American wrote in the late 1890s: 'Indeed I can say *Eureka* (I have found it), the gem of all my travel in four continents.' Another traveller asked if the picturesque glacier on the nearby mountain was real – or had it been put there by the CPR?

If the mountains attracted visitors they also created problems as crews, rotary and side plows worked to clear the winter's snow, and locomotives struggled to haul freight trains up the Big Hill. Between 1885 and 1911, avalanches killed over 200 people. Thirty-one snowsheds had been built along a 12-mile stretch in Rogers Pass. On 1 February 1899 a slide wiped out the station there, killing seven people. On 4 March 1910, as a crew cleared one snow slide, another overwhelmed them, burying and killing 62 people. In 1913, the Company began construction of the longest railway tunnel in Canada to bypass Rogers Pass. When completed in December 1916, the five-mile long Connaught Tunnel eliminated ten miles of hazards.

The war ended the Company's golden years. Never again would it dominate the west as it did during that time. In 1913, it carried 15,480,934 people. During the First World War, trains carried troops to the Atlantic ports – and contingents of Chinese labourers to support the armies in France and Flanders. CPR management and workers went into uniform and organized the railways there to supply the war fronts.

The CPR carried away to war the men of Walhacin, an Indian word for 'land of plenty.' They had irrigated land near Kamloops and made it fruitful. Storms destroyed the flumes while they were at war, and the town died.

On 11 September 1915, Van Horne died.

Saskatchewan, the car that carried the railway builder to Craigellachie 30 years earlier, formed part of his funeral train.

And on that day, every wheel on the CPR stopped for five minutes.

When they began to roll again, they moved into a very different and much more competitive world than the one in which Van Horne and Shaughnessy had nurtured and expanded the CPR.

Below and facing page: Indians show off their finery for Banff Indian Days held near CPR's Banff Springs Hotel.
World-renowned for its breathtaking location, the Banff Springs is by far CPR's most famous hotel.
Overleaf: Matthew Park photographed Canadian Expeditionary Force troops ready to entrain at Calgary in 1915.

Competition
and the
Depression Years:
1918-1939

'The shareholders and Directors of the Company have always been impressed with the idea that the interests of the Company are intimately connected with those of the Dominion, and no effort or expense has been spared to help in promoting the development of the whole continent.'

Lord Shaughnessy,
President and Chairman of the Board, 1918.

The dreamers and doers who built and ran the CPR during the high tide of Empire risked much – and gained much. George Stephen, Donald Smith, William Van Horne retired wealthy and laden with honours. Stephen, created Baron Mount Stephen, died in 1921 at the age of 92.

He and the others had found in the railway a holy cause that combined profitability and the national interest. In throwing two bands of steel across the continent they had helped to build a nation.

Writing in 1916, Keith Morris claimed that the economic history of Canada since 1885 had 'fundamentally' been the history of the Canadian Pacific. The company then operated 18,000 miles of track and 100,000 miles of telegraph line, and employed 6000 people at its Angus workshops in Montreal. In all, the Company had 120,000 men on its payroll, and about half a million people dependent on them. Another million had some concern with the Company's activities.

The Company, once viewed as a hair-brained scheme liable to go broke any minute, now represented an excellent and solid investment. In 1921, almost half the shareholders lived in Britain, and another quarter in the United States. The dividend, declared sacred, gave good, if not spectacular, returns. And the shareholders also had the feeling of being part of some great Imperial scheme for national and inter-national development.

In 1915, J B Harkin, Commissioner of Dominion Parks, illustrated how successful Van Horne's marketing of the mountains had been. Rocky Mountain National Park had 90,000 visitors. Harkin estimated that foreign tourists spent over $16 million – $13.88 an acre. Wheat exports yielded just over $74 million – $4.91 an acre of wheatland. Thus, con-

Below: This is the competition: This Canadian National 2-8-2 with a tender heaped with coal is similar to (Santa Fe) Baldwin Class Q 2-10-2.

Below: A 4-6-2 poses for its picture at Windsor, Ontario on 2 September 1954. Number 2625 would be a G-2 (light Pacific) of the 1912 series.

Above: CPR crane 414330 is parked at Coquitlam, BC, in 1952.
Below: Engine 2203 is a doughty 4-6-2 shot in Ontario, June 1942.

Below: This interesting piece of rail equipment is a CPR pile driver.

cluded Harkin, 'our export of scenery per acre . . . was equal to almost three times the acreage value of our exportable wheat surplus.' The CPR, through its irrigation schemes, had made the desert bloom. And through its tourist promotion it had made the very rocks yield dollars.

The war cut off the British tourist traffic. And when the United States entered the war in 1917, the American trade dwindled.

When anyone travelled west by train after the war, they had a choice of three transcontinental lines. The booming west and the influx of immigrants had strained the CPR system. And the Manitoba government, still concerned about the dominance of the Company and the arrogant ways of its agents, helped William Mackenzie and Donald Mann to string together railway lines in Manitoba and to expand their Canadian Northern Railway. By the end of 1902, these two men had extended their line to Thunder Bay. Then they reduced their rates for grain, forcing the CPR to do the same.

The Grand Trunk Railway under general manager Charles M Hays also eyed the bustling west. It formed a subsidiary, the Grand Trunk Pacific, and reached an agreement with Laurier's Liberals. The government would build a National Transcontinental Railway from Moncton to Winnipeg, and the Grand Trunk Pacific would carry the line from there to the Pacific. The first train on this new line reached Prince Rupert, BC, on 9 April 1914, and the National Transcontinental line between Quebec and Winnipeg opened on 1 June in the same year.

Meanwhile, Mackenzie and Mann went their merry way across the west, building the Great Northern, picking up charters and grants from anyone who wanted a railway. The last spike in their transcontinental line to Vancouver was driven in January 1915.

It soon became obvious that traffic could not sustain three lines across Canada. The *Grain Growers Guide,* no friend of the Company, noted on 9 May 1917:

The CPR is one of the finest railway systems under the sun. It is well financed, well operated and gives good service with enormous profits to its shareholders, totalling last year [1916] $49,000,000. The loss on all other railways was only $20,000,000.

Below: This dramatic shot depicts a 4-6-2 in Winnipeg, Manitoba. The cloud of smoke pours from the locomotive just behind.

Bottom: This CPR excursion car was photographed in Vancouver, BC in July 1952.
Opposite bottom: Two CPR workers, apparently at their leisure, peer at the photographer of a passenger car at Cranbook, British Columbia.

Above: Sir Edward Beatty, Shaughnessy's successor, originally joined CPR as a lawyer who fought to keep CPR a privately-owned corporation. A lifelong bachelor, he dedicated all his time to the railroad.

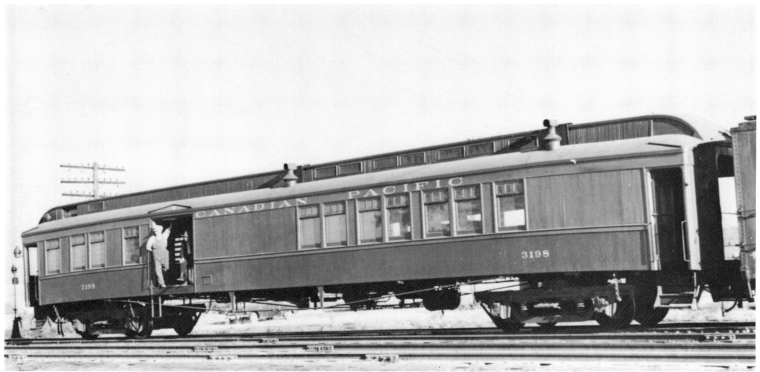

A cartoon portrayed the CPR as a fat, bejewelled pig; the other railways appeared as scrawny porkers. Shaughnessy had a simple solution to this problem. The government should nationalize all three railways – and let the CPR manage the combined venture.

Shaughnessy retired on 11 October, 1918, handing over the presidency to Edward Beatty, the first native-born Canadian to hold the post. Son of the first manager of the Company's Great Lakes steamers, Beatty had joined the CPR as a lawyer and risen rapidly through the ranks.

A photograph of Beatty, probably taken in 1919, shows him standing next to the Prince of Wales on the deck of a ship. The prince looks withdrawn, standing with hand in pocket, heels together. Beatty has a prizefighter's stance, feet apart, hands at side, hat tipped over his right eye, a slight smile on his face and a cigar clutched firmly in his left hand. It's almost as if the Company had wrested dominion over Canada from the Royal Family, its rightful rulers.

Beatty, a Presbyterian, liked the 'idea of a one man organization.' A lonely man, Beatty filled the bachelor day of his life with the Company. 'It's too bad that Ed married the CPR' one of his few friends observed.

The Company needed all the attention that Beatty could offer.

In 1922, the government had created the Canadian National Railway out of the bankrupt messes of other lines. The CPR now had a rival with access to the public purse. During the reign of Beatty, many governments took over their national railway systems to protect the public interest. But Beatty remained a foe of state ownership of industry. In one speech he claimed: 'Canadian corporations are good citizens, and so long as they are guided by men of ability and with ideals, they will not only continue to be good citizens, but will develop from within themselves thousands of men whose standards of citizenship are unconsciously elevated through that association.'

Allied with this rather mystical approach was an increased stress by Beatty on attracting traffic to the line. In 1919, the *TransCanada Limited,* a luxury, all-sleeper train, began its run, and in the 1920s, the *Toronto Express* and the *Mountaineer* from Chicago whisked travellers west.

Beatty encouraged settlement, assisting returning soldiers in Alberta and Saskatchewan to set up 320-acre farms. In 1922-23, the Company settled on their lands 2400 'clean, hard-working, thrifty 'Menonnites who had fled from Russia. In the same year, Beatty helped a group of Scottish Catholics

Opposite left: This 1912-series ten-wheeler type 4-6-2 was shot at Lambeton, Ontario, in March 1947.
Opposite right: Locomotive 2716, a 4-6-2 G-5, was photographed in Vancouver, British Columbia in 1951.
Below: This photograph of the Revelstoke station, British Columbia, was taken on a hazy day in the 1920's.

to establish the Clan Donald settlement in Vermilion, Alberta. He also tampered with the Crow Rate, receiving a blast from the *Manitoba Free Press* when he issued new rates about 'this conspiracy to break the law, rob the people and bulldoze Parliament.'

Through the 1920s, automobiles cut into the Company's short-haul traffic. But they also brought guests to the CPR hotels. For those who could not afford to stay in these hotels, the Company started mountain camps at $5.50 a day. The first, at Wapta Lake in Kicking Horse Pass, was set up in 1921. Three years later, the first annual trail ride, another tourist attraction, set out from Yoho Valley Camp.

A remarkable public relations man put a new face on the Company during the 1920s as it sought to attract travellers. John Murray Gibbon promoted the CPR with style and elegance, basing his approach on a concept of Canada far removed from the Imperial Dominion favoured by past presidents. Educated at Aberdeen, Oxford, and in Germany, Gibbon came to Canada in 1913 to work for the CPR. He

devised slogans like 'The Canadian Pacific Rockies' and 'Canadian Pacific Spans the World.' He commissioned posters and pamphlets of grace and taste. He encouraged Canadian culture, urging the CPR to involve more French Canadians in its activities. At the opening of the new wing of the Chateau Frontenac in 1926, traditional folksingers performed at a dinner for newspaper editors. In the following year the hotel was the site of the first Annual Folksong and Handicraft Festival. In 1927 Gibbon also organized a Highland Gathering and Scottish Musical Festival at Banff Springs Hotel on Labour Day. It featured a kilted clergyman, the Reverend Charles W Gordon (the novelist Ralph Connor) preaching an outdoor sermon.

At the celebration of the 50th anniversary of Confederation in Britain in 1927, Beatty heard Stanley Baldwin, the Prime Minister, claim that: 'The glory of the Canadian Pacific is that it is a corporation with a soul.' It also had lots of money, some of which it spent on purchasing ships in Britain for its fleet.

Baldwin's lofty rhetoric and the supply of ready cash that the Company seemed always able to command did little to help the CPR in a world plunged into depression in the 1930s. In November 1931 the Canadian Government set up a Royal Commission on Railways and Transportation which reported in September 1932. The CPR and the CNR, the Commission concluded, had engaged in costly and unnecessary competition with 'duplication of passenger trains . . . identical schedules . . . wasteful practices . . . establishment of a standard of passenger travel beyond the requirements of the country.' The report rejected nationalization of amalgamation, in case it created a railway monopoly. Beatty stumped the country proposing that one system under one management could solve the economic problems of the railways. He pointed out that personal income taxes had yielded the federal government $249-million over a ten-year period – 'less than half the deficit of the government railways.' The government suggested that the survival of Canada's railways lay in co-operation if necessary, but not necessarily in co-operation. The CNR continued to be propped up by the federal government while the CPR had to meet the tests of private enterprise.

Railways had been the symbol of progress in the past.

Now, as rootless, unemployed men clung to the freights, they became symbols of depression and economic stagnation. On 28 September 1930 the CPR station on Yonge Street in Toronto, completed in 1916, closed. This elegant building had marble-covered walls and a 140-foot high clock tower – but not enough passenger traffic to justify its existence. The Company had its worst year in 1932, showing a deficit of $42,000. In 1933, loans of $40 million fell due, with a further $20 million due in the following year. The banks, including the Bank of Montreal, of which Beatty was a director, demanded security to renew the loans. The president asked Prime Minister Bennett for a guarantee of a five-year loan at 5 percent in May 1933, and the government provided this under the Railway Relief Act in that year.

In the winter of 1932, the CPR closed its shops in Calgary. But the Company, in the words of James Gray in *The Winter Years,* 'stood out like a gigantic gas flare' on the prairies because of its enlightened land policy. Mortgage companies evicted farmers, then sold their farms for a fraction of what the owners owed. The CPR did not foreclose, and even cancelled interest on its loans in two years when the crops failed. The Company paid its workers as much for a day as government relief programs did for a week's work. But it demanded that the federal government enforce the Railway Act and remove the 'On-to-Ottawa' trekkers who had hoped to ride the Company's freights from Vancouver to Ottawa in 1935.

In the early 1930s, the CPR and CNR co-operated in providing work to alleviate unemployment. They also abandoned 517 miles of track, and saved $1,771,635 through joint efforts between 1935 and 1938.

In the late 1920s and through the 1930s, the CPR ran special ski trains in Ontario and Québec. But in 1937, despite increased attendance at the Canadian National Exhibition in Toronto, the number of railway passengers declined.

Canadian Pacific Facts and Figures, issued in that year, named the cause of the railway's difficulties.

> Within the past few years, and particularly the last decade, there has been a decided change in the sources from which emanate the movement of passengers by rail, due to the advent and development of new modes of transportation, chiefly that of the private automobile.

Beatty, knighted in 1935, saw the CPR experience one brief shining moment of glory before the world descended into war. In 1939, King George VI and Queen Elizabeth crossed Canada by CPR. The king, impressed by the powerful Hudson locomotives that hauled the royal train, permitted the Company to rename them 'Royal Hudsons' – and to carry crowns on the runningboards of 45 of them.

A stroke felled Beatty on 17 March 1941, robbing him of speech. News of the stroke was kept from the public as he struggled painfully back to health, trying to keep on top of company business. Vice-president D'Alton C Coleman took over more and more duties, becoming CPR's fifth president in May 1942.

Less than a year later, Edward Beatty, who had made the Company his life, died in March 1943, aged 65.

Left: Sicamous Station in British Columbia, built of wood in a board and batten style, has an air of tranquility.
Below: A CPR baggage car is parked between two boxcars in Sutherland.

The End of an Era:

The Second World War and the Passing of Steam

'A railway is a republic and a monarchy. It is a republic because there is no pre-emption of high office for any favoured class among its servants. It is a monarchy in the virtual dictatorship of its President.'

David Hanna, *Trains of Recollection*, 1926

Only too often the history of the CPR emerges as the story of businessmen like Stephen and Beatty battling against great odds to complete a transcontinental railway and to keep it running. The thousands of men who built and operated the line, and those whose lives it touched and changed are more than footnotes to these 'great lives.' For the most part they have remained faceless and mute.

One pioneer called the CPR 'the mighty monster of the west,' and described the railroad big shots as a 'bunch of pirates.' But he added that they got the job done. Another man took over a station in 1906, receiving $35 a month, plus a house for $5 a month and free oil and kerosene. When he retired in 1947, he was earning $165 a month. Railroading ran in the blood in some families, all of whose members worked for the CPR over five generations. One man recalled the time he wanted to become a railroader. He went out to Medicine Hat on a railway pass to a job as a wiper at the roundhouse in 1903. He was expected to work for 11 hours for $1.21. When he found that his room and board would cost him $1 a day, he decided to seek work elsewhere.

The Company provided steady work, and treated its workers well. It created a social structure in which everyone knew his place, and its workers took pride in belonging to such a famous company. At midnight on 5 August 1925, engineman Seth Partridge's train, on its way up the Big Hill, ran into a rock and clay slide. He ran down the hill to Yoho station, and warned the occupants, who left the building a few seconds before the slide wiped it out. The grateful Company named a sliding after Partridge.

David Hanna, the first president of the Canadian National, summed up another appeal of railroading as a way of life when he claimed that any of his company's 100,000 person workforce would find 'the highest executive office is open' – if

Below: Brute force clothed in steel: this locomotive, a 4-6-2, is a Pacific type of the heavier G-3 or G-4 class.
Bottom: The sun sets at Midway, British Columbia. The peaceful and glorious view is on the Kettle Valley Route.

A vacationers' train arrives at Banff, Alberta.

he 'entered the service young enough.' In the 1920s, D C Carleton, who started with the CPR as a clerk in the baggage department in 1887, had made it to vice-president.

Women did not play a significant role in the all-male world of railroading. Kate Reed, wife of Hayter Reed, Manager-in-Chief of the Company's hotel department in the first years of this century, decorated the hotels with quiet elegance. And a faithful secretary helped Edward Beatty to handle Company affairs after his stroke in 1941.

An ex-employee reported that there was 'a paternal approach mixed with authoritarianism' in the Company's management style, adding that it resembled being in the military: 'Everyone knew their rank and the guy above was God.' Even fairly recently, an executive was told by the president that 'we own you twenty-four hours a day.'

On the line, the gods at the top of the pantheon were the conductor and the engineer. As early as 1895, a commentator noted:

> Like Japan and ancient Sparta, the cars are subject to a species of 'dual monarch,' the parallel potentates being the conductor — who generally retires with a fortune nobody knows how, for he doesn't get tipped — and the Negro conductor.

Blacks found jobs with the railway as porters and sleeping car attendants, but seldom rose above these ranks.

A CPR passenger train became a world unto itself as it crossed the country. The conductor, the 'captain of the ship' and the 'Lord Mayor' of a 'city on wheels' wore a watch that might cost a month's pay as his badge of office. The conductor looked after the paper work, wore a suit, and ensured that the train arrived and left on time. Tensions often developed between this white collar worker, the supreme authority on the train, and the engineer, known as the hogger and always addressed as 'Mister.' The engineer also earned a top wage, but he wore overalls and worked with his hands.

In 1931, conductors received the highest wages in Canada. In Moose Jaw, another CPR creation, in which it invested $5 million for railway facilities, conductors and engineers lived in big houses. But the railway superintendent occupied a mansion.

Hand in hand with autocracy went paternalism.

Beatty heard of an engineer who was due to retire without ever having seen him. He arranged to travel on the man's train. At the end of the section, Beatty went up to the cab, introduced himself, and wished the engineer a happy retirement.

The railroad created new skills, rituals, symbols.

A man known as the 'bank' fireman started a fire under the engine in the roundhouse: It took about an hour and a half for a locomotive to raise steam. The engineer would arrive an hour ahead of time to fuss over the locomotive, wiping it down with a piece of waste, polishing the bell. The CPR took great pride in its shining engines. The engineer controlled the locomotive with throttle and brake, from the right side of the cab. The fireman looked out of the left window for any signals, and rang the bell. Some firemen could not talk to their engineers — unless they spoke first. A fireman might work for ten years or more before being promoted to engineer. He had to handle the scoop to keep an even fire burning. A run of 120 miles would consume 12 to 15 tons of coal, depending

A CPR 4-6-2 puffs out of Winnipeg, Manitoba, heading west.

on track and weather conditions. On the 150 miles between Revelstoke, BC, and Lake Louise, one CPR fireman emptied the tender three times, shovelling 30 tons of coal on an eight hour trip.

Working in the yards that began to spread over the landscape at certain places in Canada required other skills.

The yardmaster could locate any car on the miles of track, even though they changed daily. A freight conductor would watch a long string of cars move past – then take out a notebook and pencil and jot down all their numbers.

The authoritarian structure often led to casual cruelty.

One cold night in a CPR yard, a shivering young man climbed into the cab of an engine to warm himself. The engineer demanded to know what he did. When the man said that he worked the switches, the hogger told him he belonged on the ground – not in the cab – and that he should 'git.'

The passing of the trains in rural areas marked the hours of the days. 'Milk trains' stopped at every flag station through which the 'moonlights,' the crack expresses, roared. The caboose was called the 'van,' 'crummy,' 'dog house.' Local

railways received nicknames from irate travellers. The T H & B (Toronto, Hamilton and Buffalo) became 'To Hell and Back.' That line vanished into the CPR in 1977.

But no one seems to have mocked the mighty CPR with a nickname that stuck. That other great Canadian institution, the Royal Canadian Mounted Police, generated scores of movies that distorted its real world and embarrassed its officers. The CPR's activities gave rise to only one Hollywood film – Canadian Pacific – made in 1949, and starring Randolph Scott and Jane Wyatt.

The CPR developed increasingly powerful locomotives. To haul a 15-car train up the Big Hill took four heavy engines. This problem was eased in August 1909, when the spiral tunnels between Field and Hector doubled the length of the track, and halved the grade.

The 4-4-0 locomotives (four wheels in front, four driving wheels, no wheels under the cab) dominated the first decades of the railways. In 1889, the CPR, which had used a wide range of locomotive types, built the first Ten-Wheeler, a 4-6-0, and over the years operated almost 1000 of them. Competition among transcontinental lines led to the develop-

ment of faster and faster trains. The *Atlantics,* acquired by the CPR, had 84-inch driving wheels. Between 1906 and 1946 the Company used the first modern steam locomotives, the *Pacifics,* with large cylinders and boiler capacity and powerful traction to haul trains weighing up to 500 tons. Then came the *Mikados* that proved to be outstanding successes at hauling heavy loads up steep grades. The handsome *Hudsons,* later streamlined, came into operation in 1929 as did the mighty *Selkirks,* used extensively in the Rockies. The first *Jubilee* with 80-inch driving wheels, was 'outshopped' by the Montreal Locomotive Works in 1936.

The fast and stopping trains that crossed Canada changed the lives and perception of many people. The luxury trains had electricity, running hot and cold water, elegant restaurants and parlour cars — comforts conspicuously lacking in most of the houses and communities through which they roared. The trains broke down the isolation of settlers, as the stations became the focus of community life. Time and the hours took on a new meaning. The comings and goings of the trains drew businessmen and idlers to the station to see who was arriving — and who was leaving town.

People came to pick up the papers and the mail, to hear the latest gossip from inside and outside the community. The Morse and telegraph keys chattered away, sending messages across the land, passing the signals that kept the trains running on time. The train stopped for a minute or two to drop off the mail, express parcels and passengers. Then the lordly conductor shouted 'All aboard,' and swung on to the train which steamed away, driving rods flailing, wheels turning, steam escaping.

To youngsters, the train represented power, escape and excitement, reminding them of faraway places beyond the horizon. It brought the city to small communities and lured away their youth. Everyone knew the language of the loco-motive's whistle. A short shriek meant that brakes were being applied to stop the train, a long one that the train was nearing a station, junction or crossing. On the prairies the whistle broke the isolation of farmers: some people could tell the temperature from the way the whistle cut through the cold air. People set their watches by the trains as they became symbols of regularity and reliability.

People on the local lines developed an affection for 'their'

trains and 'their' crews. One CPR railroader recalled that they'd let people off at their homes, stop for dinner and even sit on a bridge and fish. An old couple in Ontario waited at a stop with turkey legs for the CPR crew one Christmas Day.

In December 1937 an event cast its shadow over the CPR. It acquired its first diesel-electric unit for use in rail yards. These power units cost more to buy – but less to operate.

During the Second World War, freight tonnage rose as trucks, gasoline and rubber shortages developed. The Angus shops in Montreal turned out Valentine tanks as well as Hudson locomotives, and the government took over 22 of the Company's ships; twelve were sunk in action. Passengers returned to the trains. In 1939, the CPR carried 7.2 million passengers. In 1944, the number had risen to 18.4 million, the highest ever reached by the system. Overall railway revenues doubled between 1939 and 1945. The war effort strained the CPR system. In 1939, it had 48,689 employees. By 1945, they numbered 70,775, despite the enlistment of 20,742 in the Canadian forces.

In 1941, the government froze wages and freight rates. Not until 1944 did it grant railway workers a six cents-an-hour wage increase, and a bonus. Operating expenses on the railway soared, and after the end of the war, highway carriers began to compete for freight. Price and wage controls ended in 1946, but rates and fares on the CPR remained at the old levels. In 1948, the Board of Transport Commissioners granted a general increase in tolls, but could not raise the rates on export grain because of the sanctity of the Crow Rate. Wage rates, material costs and, after 1957, interest rates, rose steadily while it became apparent that freight and passenger traffic had almost reached their ceilings.

The Company responded to these new stresses by modernizing and diversifying.

The grumbling, growling, hooting diesel replaced the shrieking, thundering steam locomotives under the direction of Norris 'Buck' Crump, Company president from 1955 to 1964 and chairman until 1972. His very name sounded like the slamming of a door on the romantic era of railroading.

At one time, railroaders had been the élite of the Canadian labour force, and their unions became very conservative. But

Ian Sinclair, who reigned as president from 1966 to 1972, the Company showed how innovative and inventive it could be in responding to change. It installed computers, bought and ran dayliners, built container terminals, developed 'unit' and 'robot' trains, studied railway electrification west of Calgary, introduced piggybacking (carrying highway trailers on flat cars), automated its marshalling yards, acquired modern locomotives and new rolling stock for many specialized uses.

As machines replaced men, the old sense of pride and identity of the railroaders began to crumble. One complained that standardization of equipment, computerization and the use of radio communications had taken responsibility out of the hands of engineers. Before modernization, the CPR workers – and especially the engineers – felt they were in charge. The loss of autonomy was reflected in an increased feeling that somebody was looking over people's shoulders, checking up on them.

In 1948 a national railway strike appeared inevitable. The unions wanted a 25 cents-an-hour wage increase, and the companies offered 10 cents. Crump, apparently swayed by the argument that only Russia would benefit from a railway strike, compromised at 17 cents. In 1950, Canada suffered its first national rail strike over the issue of wages. Technological change triggered other disputes. On 2 January 1957, 65,000 CPR employees walked out in support of 2850 firemen who felt threatened by dieselization. The union claimed that firemen were indispensable for safety reasons, the government ordered the men back, and the resulting enquiry showed that firemen were reduntant on diesels. The firemen struck again in 1958, but received no backing from other unions and swiftly settled for what they could gain from a company bent on preserving its profits.

On 3 July 1971, the Company changed its name from the Canadian Pacific Railway Company to Canadian Pacific Limited to accommodate its varied transportation and natural resource activities.

The Company had already changed its symbol and its slogan. Through the years it favoured a simple shield with the words 'Canadian Pacific' on it. From 1886 to 1929 a strange-looking beaver sat atop the shield. The beaver dropped off in 1929, and the slogan 'World's Greatest Travel System' appeared on the shield. The beaver made a comeback in 1946, with a new slogan; 'Spans the World.' In 1963, the Company motto became: 'Diversification is the key to Canadian Pacific's progress.' In 1968, the shield and the beaver gave way up to abstract symbol still in use. The initials 'CP' were stylized, and the symbol combines 'a triangle, suggesting motion or direction, a segment of a circle suggesting global activities and a portion of a square suggesting stability.' (See pages 10 and 11.)

The Company no longer has its former clear-cut identity. It now engages in many activities. It has dumped its passengers. And a generation has grown up unaware of the Company's history and of the great power it wielded.

Throughout its history, the Company has played a significant role in uniting Canadians. A writer in the 1920s pointed out another feature of the Company – its sense of 'high moral purpose.' He told of Gideon Swain, the general custodian at Winnipeg, who rounded on two 'smart men' who were swearing in his station while women and children boarded a train.

In a speech in 1980, Ian Sinclair, CP's president, neatly summarized the Company's priorities: 'The first corporate obligation is to earn a profit.'

Locomotive No 5310 pushes a snow plow in East Coulee, Alberta.

after the war, discontent arose among the CPR workers, who realized that past glory and company spirit offered no recompense for rising living costs. Crump, son of a CPR employee in Revelstoke, BC, joined the Company as an apprentice machinist at 16, and claimed he'd worn overalls longer than most union leaders. He wrote his thesis in engineering on diesels and presided over their widescale adoption by the railway. The first road (main line) diesels went into service in 1948-49. By 1954, about one third of freight and passenger trains were being hauled by diesels. By 1960, 'dieselization' had been completed, and in that year the last steam locomotive to pull a train on CP rail lines hauled a special from Montreal to St Lin and back. It was a 4-4-0, built in 1887.

The diesels allowed runthroughs. They had no need of coal and water. So communities built to serve the steam trains simply lost their reason for being and began to vanish.

During Crump's tenure, and that of his successor, lawyer

A big 4-6-2 steam locomotive, engineer peeking from the cab, standing in Abbotsford, British Columbia, on a crisp March day in 1943.

Canadian Pacific's Ships and Planes

'The CPR was on the Pacific shore; but there was no traffic with the orient . . . The first CPR steamer from Vancouver to Asia carried two carloads of shingles and the bodies of several Chinamen piously being returned to their ancestral sepulchres.'

David Hanna, *Trains of Recollections*, 1926

From the beginning of his involvement with the railway, George Stephen had a vision of an all-British route to the Far East, a transportation system stretching from Liverpool to Hong Kong. In 1882 the Company issued a map showing steamship connections to Japan and Hong Kong from its western terminus. Three years later the CPR tendered a bid to the British Post Office to carry the mail fortnightly between Vancouver and Hong Kong for £100,000, but the offer was rejected.

Despite this rebuff, the Company chartered seven sailing ships to carry cargo from the Far East to its Pacific railhead. The first of these, the 800-ton wooden barque *W B Flint*, docked at Port Moody on 27 July 1886, with a million pounds of tea consigned to Hamilton, Toronto and New York. The connecting train sped across the country to deliver the tea to New York only 49 days after the ship left Yokohama. Between August 1886 and January 1887 the other chartered ships did the 'tea run,' providing 4000 tons of freight for the new railway.

The Company then acquired the *Abyssinia, Batavia* and *Parthia*, ex-Cunard steamers, under charter. The *Abyssinia*, out of Hong Kong and Yokohama, tied up at the new CPR wharf in Vancouver on 14 June 1887. It carried 22 first class passengers and 80 Chinese in steerage, three sacks of mail, 11 packages of newspapers and almost 3000 tons of cargo, most of it tea consigned to Chicago and New York. Later in the season, the chartered ships carried the British Minister to Japan and the brother of the King of Siam. From its beginning, the Company strove to attract distinguished travellers to its ships.

The first season resulted in a loss for the Company.

But it plunged on into the shipping business. In 1889 it placed orders for three 6000-ton vessels – the first 'Empresses' of India, China and Japan. With graceful, yacht-like lines, and excellent service, these fast passenger vessels soon gave the Canadian Pacific the same reputation on the

ocean as its passenger trains did on land. And they proved profitable.

The *Empress of India* ran her trials in January 1891, decked out with the red-and-white checked flag that Van Horne had designed (see illustration, page 10). These new ships carried mail between Vancouver and China and Japan under a £60,000 contract secured by the Company in 1890. The contract carried a penalty clause that was never invoked in the first 15 years of operation.

David Brown, the Company's representative in the Far East, showed the same aggressive drive that marked so many of the CPR management. He secured connections with Australia and New Zealand – 'hands across the sea and let the kangaroo shake hands with the beaver.' He lured traffic from Ceylon by telling a senior government official: 'I represent the Canadian Pacific Railway, and I can give you transportation right into the exhibition grounds in Chicago' so that the country could participate in the World's Fair there in 1894.

The Company made plans in 1884 for a link across the Atlantic. On 29 January 1886 Stephen wrote to Sir John A Macdonald, after talking with Andrew Allan of the ship-owning family.

He now knows that nothing but the very best and fastest ships will be of any use to us, and that whoever owns them, the CPR must have a substantial control over them so as to ensure a unity of action . . .

Quality, integration of services, and unity of action became the marks of the Company style as it entered the golden years. As the railway penetrated the lake country of southern British Columbia, the CPR built steamers to connect branch lines. The first of these, the *Aberdeen,* came out of the CPR's own shipyard at Okanagan Landing in May 1894. In 1901 the Company secured control of the Canadian Pacific Navigation Company, and the red-and-white flag went up on a fleet of 14 steamers that plied the coastal waters of British Columbia. In 1903 the *Princess Victoria,* the first of the new company's specially designed ships, began to win the hearts of the people on the west coast with her grace and speed.

In the same year, Shaughnessy bought 15 passenger and cargo ships from the Elder Dempster Lines. The Company also moved into the emigration business, offering steerage passage between Liverpool and Quebec and Montreál for £5 10s; the immigrant ships carried cattle to London on the return trip. In 1906 the *Empress of Britain,* the first of the

The *Abyssinia* was launched on 3 March 1870 by J & G Thomson, Clydebank, for the Cunard Line and taken over by the builders in 1880 as partial payment for the *Servia & Catalonia.* S B Guion bought the vessel and installed compound engines in 1882. Ownership was transferred in 1885 to Sir William Pearce. On 11 January 1887 the *Abyssinia* was obtained for the CP Pacific service. On 28 January 1887 she departed Vancouver on her 17th, and last, CPR voyage. In October of 1891 she reverted to the Guion Steamship Co Ltd. On 18 December 1891 she was destroyed by a fire at sea, but, happily, her passengers were picked up by the Norddeutscher Lloyd steamer *Spree.*

A sizeable crowd gathers to welcome the Duke and Duchess of Connaught as they arrive on the *Abyssinia* in May 1890. This Vancouver Harbour scene also includes the CP Navigation Co's *Premier,* docked on the left. Note the dismounted cannons lying on the quay in the lower left corner of the picture. To the right carriages wait to drive passengers to their hotels.

Atlantic 'Empresses,' began its run on that ocean. Three years later, the Company absorbed the Allan Line in a secret deal.

The very high standards set by the Company for its ships proved to be a liability when the First World War broke out. The fast ships of the Atlantic and Pacific fleets were taken over by the government for use as transports or auxiliary cruisers. When the first Canadian contingent sailed for England in October 1914, 13 of the 31 liners in the convoy had once sailed under the flags of the Company or the Allan Line. About a dozen CPR ships were lost to enemy action during the First World War. Immigration, of course, dropped considerably. In 1913, 400,870 people arrived in Canada. Two years later, the number of immigrants had dropped to 36,665.

In the 1920s, the Company profited by meeting national needs in Canada, which wanted to fill its empty spaces, and in Britain, which wanted to empty its crowded cities. Reduced fares attracted British immigrants seeking to start a new life in a new world. The Company carried 11,000 'harvesters' across the Atlantic and Canada to work on the farms in the west.

The ships, like the railway, created their own social structure.

In 1927 the company built the four 'Duchess' passenger ships. They tended to roll and were known as the 'Drunken Duchesses.' A man who served on the *Duchess of York* wrote later about the lives of the 200 crew who served the needs of

Above: The *Empress of Canada III* steams proudly. The 650 foot liner was launched on 10 May 1960 by Vickers Armstrong Ship Builders Ltd, Walker on Tyne. The ship served with CP from 1961 to 1972 when she began service with the Carnaval Cruise Line as the *Mardi Gras.*
Right: A CP Ships container ship plows ahead with a full load. Containerization has revolutionized shipping since its introduction. A cargo can be shipped intact in a sturdy container from its point of origin to its final destination.

the 1570 passengers these ships could carry.

Kitchen boys received slightly more than £3 a month, and assistant cooks slightly more than £7. Uniforms were not supplied nor was laundry done free, except when the ship was in Canada. The chef had his private room, and the senior staff lived above the water line in 'Tin Town.' The rest of the catering and service staff crowded into a honeycomb of 'glory holes' near the ship's bows. The working day began at 5:45 am and ended at 11 pm when the chef said, 'the rest of the day is your own . . .' The night before the ship docked, everyone stayed up to clean and polish everything, for in those days, 'you never took a dirty ship into port.' If the ship tied up at one minute to midnight, everyone lost the next day's pay.

Despite these conditions, the spirit on board was 'fantastic.'

Over the years, the Company operated a wide range of ships from luxury passenger liners to tugs. Many came to grief. The *Empress of Ireland,* rammed by the Norwegian collier *Storstad* in the St Lawrence on the foggy night of 29 May 1914, took over 1000 people to their deaths when she

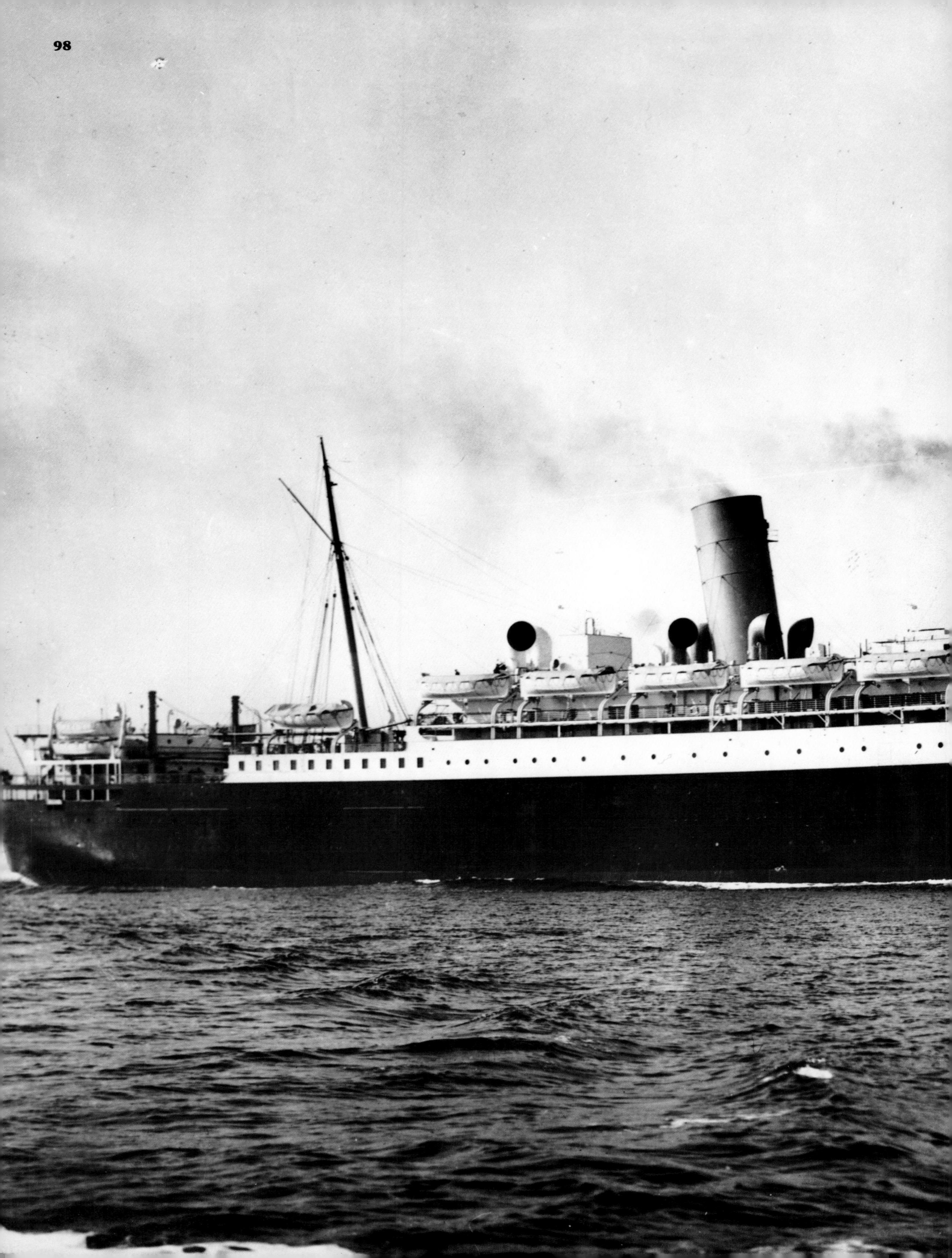

The Duchess of York was launched by John Brown & Co Ltd, Clydebank on 28 September 1928. On 22 March 1929 she sailed from Liverpool on her maiden voyage. In 1940 she was requisitioned to serve as a troopship and on 11 July 1943 she was sunk by enemy aircraft off the coast of Morocco, joining the roll of stout CP ships to be lost in her country's service.

The CP tanker *Fort Garry* steadily plows toward her destination. Note the safety warnings painted on the bridge superstructure which are necessary, given the highly flammable nature of her cargo.

sank in fifteen minutes. On 23 October 1918, the *Princess Sophia,* southbound from Skagway down the Inner Passage of Alaska, went aground on the Vanderbilt Reef. The ship seemed securely wedged on the rocks, so most of the 343 passengers and crew went to bed. A sudden gale lifted the ship's stern, and she slid off the reef into the water, taking everyone to their deaths. Only a dog survived.

In October 1940 the largest and most luxurious ship in the Company fleet, *The Empress of Britain,* sailing alone off northwestern Ireland on military duties, was attacked by a bomber. The blazing ship, towed by a tug, became the target of a U-boat, which sank her with two torpedoes.

By the early 1960s, air travel had cut into the Company's transocean passenger trade. The third *Empress of Britain,* commissioned in 1956, ended her service with the Company eight years later by being sold to a Greek shipping line. In 1960 the Company launched its last passenger liner, the *Empress of Canada.* Although the CPR generated money by using its passenger liners on cruises during the winter, the fate of the *Empress of Canada* showed that such ships had no future. Only 20 people – including three CP officials – saw this beautiful ship leave her pier at Montreal on 18 November 1971. She carried 300 passengers in a space designed for 1000. Sold to an American cruise line, she became the *Mardi Gras* in 1972.

Cargo carrying proved to be more profitable – if less glamorous. In 1964, the Company ordered the *Beaverbrook,* a 6000-ton cargo carrier, the first CP ship specifically designed to carry containers. Seven years later the first of the new 'cellular' ships with the 'CP' designator came into operation. Displacing 14,000 tons, the *CP Discoverer, CP Trade* and *CP Voyageur* could carry 700 containers.

In 1964, as its ocean shipping activities contracted, the Company created Canadian Pacific (Bermuda) Ltd to own, operate and charter oceangoing bulk carriers. The new company's fleet expanded rapidly in the 1970s. Tankers and VLCC (Very Large Cargo Carriers) carried the names of *R B Angus, Lord Mount Stephen* and *Lord Strathcona.* One was christened with the name of that bulky railway builder, *W C Van Horne.* They sailed into troubled waters in the 1980s as more and more ships chased fewer and fewer cargoes. The Company learned the hard way that big was no longer beautiful – or even profitable. The bulk shipping operation turned a profit of $44 million in 1981 — but lost $40.9 million in 1983. In that year, CP Ships lost a total of $74.3 million.

Poor economic conditions forced the Company into joint ventures. At the end of 1983, it reorganized its container operations, and withdrew from service between the United States East Coast and Western Europe. On 1 January 1984 Canadian Pacific and Compagnie Maritime Belge formed a joint venture to compete more effectively in the container trade between Montreal and Western Europe.

* * *

Although the Canadian Pacific Railway received permission from the government in 1919 to own and operate commercial aircraft inside and outside Canada, it did nothing about taking to the air until 1930. Then it cooperated with Canadian National Railways and invested half a million dollars in Canadian Airways Ltd, which consisted of a number of local lines. When C D Howe became Minister of Transportation in 1936, with jurisdiction over civil aviation, he made it very plain that he wanted no competition for his new Crown corporation, Trans-Canada Airlines. So the CPR

looked north, and acquired 10 bush airlines with 77 aircraft in 1941-42. Canadian Pacific Air Lines thus came into being on 1 January 1942.

Blending together a wild crew of northern pilots who flew by the seat of their pants (and ran their companies the same way) and a staid and conservative railway gave the Company both flexibility and stability. It was thus able to make an effective contribution to Canada's war effort in the air. The Canadian Pacific operated air observer schools for the British Commonwealth Air Training Plan, overhauled aircraft for the RCAF, and helped to establish and operate the North West Staging Route for planes flying to Alaska and Russia.

Along with one of the companies it bought, CP Air Lines acquired Grant McConachie, president of Yukon Southern. McConachie did for the Company, in the air, what Van Horne did for the railway on land. He had the energy and instincts of a maverick, disciplined by first hand knowledge of flying in Canada's north where a single mistake could be fatal. Born in 1909, the son of a CNR railroader, McConachie grew up in Edmonton. An unruly youth, he ran away from home at 16 to join the Canadian Navy. Then he worked for the railway until he found an outlet for his energy in flying. By 1931 he had accumulated enough time in the air to qualify as a commercial pilot. McConachie had an uncle who started out to be a fireman. The engineer had told him to shovel more coal, whereupon the uncle had opened the fire door, thrown in the shovel and left a career in railroading for the life of a huckster selling magic medicinal remedies. This uncle

Below: The CP Ship *Voyageur* was launched by Cammell Laird & Co, Birkenhead on 19 August 1970.
Opposite: CP Air's DC-10s were built in Long Beach by McDonnell Douglas.

agreed to provide the capital to put his nephew into the airline business. Soon McConachie was piloting the single Fokker aircraft that made up the fleet of Independent Airways through the Rockies, hauling freight between Vancouver and Edmonton. The business did not thrive, so McConachie flew fish out of northern lakes, founding Yukon Southern in 1939. He survived a bad crash, never made much money from his planes, but sustained himself through incredible luck and a great deal of nerve. A man with a perpetual grin, McConachie combined the skills of a bush pilot with the vision of an international entrepreneur. He became the prime mover of CP Air Lines' efforts in supplying the North West Staging Route, the Alaska Highway, and the Canol Project which took oil from the Norman Wells field in the Mackenzie Valley to Whitehorse in the Yukon.

In 1946, McConachie moved to Montreal as assistant to the President of CP Air Lines, helping to turn it from a string of bush lines into a major scheduled international and domestic carrier. On 11 February 1947 he became president of the company — and convinced Canadian Pacific to move the airline's headquarters to Vancouver in the following year.

Canadian Pacific Air Lines made its inaugural flight from Vancouver to Sydney, via Honolulu and Fiji, on 10 July 1949. The Labour Government in Australia had been reluctant to grant landing rights to a capitalist corporation. McConachie showed the Prime Minister, a former engine driver, his union card, told him he was a 'brother of the plates,' and secured the rights.

The airline expanded its services to Tokyo and Hong Kong in September 1949, just in time to cash in on the immigrant traffic from the Crown Colony. The Korean conflict also generated a great deal of traffic for the airline; its reputation

for good service and quality attracted American officers who wanted to fly across the Pacific in comfort. In the 1950s, Canadian Pacific Air Lines began scheduled flights to New Zealand, Mexico, Lima, Buenos Aires and Santiago, and then to Lisbon and Madrid. The planes, called *White Empresses,* maintained the tradition of service and comfort of the Company's great ocean liners.

In a strange reversal of history, Canadians began to praise the airline's service, comparing it most favourably with the government's airline that had a monopoly of scheduled passenger flights across Canada. The Canadian Pacific had struggled hard to link Canadians by rail. It had been criticized for becoming a monopoly. Now it came up against a firm government monopoly of air traffic across Canada. The Air Transport Board turned down the airline's applications to launch a transcontinental service on the grounds that it was not in the public interest to have competition.

McConachie persisted. On 4 May 1959 CP Air Lines initiated its service across Canada, giving up some of its northern routes outside the Yukon to a regional carrier. In 1961, however, the airline lost $7.6 million. It slowly moved into the black, earning a profit of $7.2 million in 1965.

McConachie had burned his candle at both ends – and in the middle – to make a success of CP Air Lines. He died of a heart attack in Long Beach, California, on 29 June 1965, but he had lived to see his airline become a power in Canada. He had heard the federal government name it as official Canadian flag carrier in the South Pacific, South America and Southeast Europe. In the same month in which he died, the government had referred to Air Canada and CP Air Lines as their 'chosen instruments' in the international aviation field.

To retain its competitive edge, the company acquired Boeing 747 jumbo jets in 1973, the same year in which it took the name CP Air. At that time, it had about 6500 employees, and flew over 50,000 miles along routes that radiated out like a large X from its headquarters in Vancouver. To the west, the airline served Hong Kong and Sydney. The line reached south to Santiago and Buenos Aires, and east to Tel Aviv. From Vancouver its planes flew south to Los Angeles and north to Whitehorse.

Stars among CP Air's galaxy of jetliners are the twin engined Boeing 737 used on short runs (above) and the huge Boeing 747, which is used on intercontinental flights (opposite).

In 1984, CP Air finally became a truly transcontinental airline. It showed its old expansionist urge by absorbing Eastern Provincial Airways, a regional carrier serving Atlantic Canada. It bought the airline from Newfoundland Capital Corporation, after a pilot's strike and intransigent management had generated a loss of $8 million in 1983.

The energy crunch of the 1970s, and the economic downturn of the 1980s, raised the airline's costs and lowered its revenues. CP Air lost $39.2 million in 1982, but cut its losses to $16.4 million in the following year.

During 1983, CP Air introduced the 'hub and spoke' system to provide greater efficiency and a more convenient schedule for passengers. It exchanged some of its aircraft for shorter-range ones. And it integrated the airline's operations with those of CP Hotels to make the division more profitable and to enhance the airline's presence in the travel and tourism market.

A Transport Department audit of CP Air, released in the summer of 1984, concluded that it is generally a 'good airline' with dedicated employees. It did have some minor problems and the audit recommended 'increased company quality control, surveillance and enforcement throughout the system,' better employee training and the development of maintenance and engineering procedures. But these problems afflicted other major corporations in Canada, the audit noted.

CP Air has become just another Canadian corporation, struggling to adapt to rapid change.

Grant McConachie was the last of Canadian Pacific's originals. He gave the airline – and the Company – a sense of flair and adventure as he struggled to establish new routes and to secure permission to take his planes across the continent.

And he gave the Company a human face – something that it lacks today. And yet its activities probably touch the lives of more Canadians than at any other time in its history.

The Canadian Pacific Today

'We don't go after major successes in this company but we avoid major failures too.'

Ian Sinclair, President of Canadian Pacific, to a questioner at the Company's Annual Meeting in 1973.

J Lorne McDougall's history of the Canadian Pacific Railway, commissioned by the Company, appeared in 1968.

In his introduction, 'Buck' Crump explained why the CPR had commissioned the work to avoid the alternative – 'something which represented the work of many hands, all striving to extract what was controversial, so that it ended up a bland, flavourless mass of facts; every fact verified and most of them of no importance.'

Such defensiveness sounded odd coming from the president of the Company. The changes in the name, slogans and logo also revealed a certain nervousness about CPR's image. During the 1960s, the state began to play an increasingly important role in the lives of Canadians. It also began to take on that air of moral righteousness that marked the CPR's attempts to help Canadian unity and development. At one time, and in many places, the CPR had been 'the only outfit in the world,' as one oldtimer put it. Now the bureaucrats looked askance at private enterprise, distrusted its ways, and became suspicious when it turned a profit.

And the Company had competition in many areas. But, as McDougall noted in a masterly understatement, the 'Canadian Pacific has never been a tidy little business.' In 1962, the Company organized Canadian Pacific Enterprises Ltd (CPE), which ran its oil and gas, mines and minerals, iron and steel, forest products, real estate and agriproduct operations. Between 1970 and 1980, the Company's assets rose sixfold and its profits increased twentyfold. In 1982 CPE moved its headquarters from Montreal to Calgary – about the time the western boom burst. By 1984, the conglomerate had $12 billion in assets. But it also had suffered from the recession.

The *Globe and Mail*'s 'Report on Business 1000' for 1984 noted that the 'sagging fortunes' of Canadian Pacific and Canadian Pacific Enterprises – 'a combination considered by many to be a fitting proxy for the entire Canadian economy' – showed just how badly the recession had hit Canada. CPE's

Above right: Two types of trucks from the vast CP Express fleet pull into a parking lot. The CP Express/CP Transport trucking empire stretches from Halifax, Nova Scotia to Nanaimo on Vancouver Island. The lines reach north to Flin Flon in Manitoba and Dawson Creek in British Columbia.

Right: Triple diesel locomotives in 'action red' haul a string of tank cars out of Montréal, Québec. Montréal is the CPR headquarters city, and also has the distinction of being the easternmost part of the railroad's line that is double-tracked.

profit fell 58.4 percent in 1983, coming to only $62.9 million on revenues of $8.7 billion. On a compounded basis, CPE's profits had declined more than 30 percent in each of the past five fiscal years. In its thrusting, expansionist way, CPE had acquired the Canadian International Paper Company for $1.1 billion (US) in 1981 – and lost $101.8 million on it in 1982.

The parent company, CP Ltd, did little better than its offspring. CP Rail earned $184 million in 1983, but CP Ships lost $74.3 million and CP Air $16.4 million. CP Ltd's profit fell 24 percent over the previous year to $143.6 million on revenue of $13.1 billion. But the Company's five-year return on capital came to 16.8 percent, a reasonably decent showing for tough economic times.

And the Company ranked first in Canada in 1983 in revenues, seventh in assets, and 19th in profits. CPE Ltd ranked fifth in revenues, tenth in assets, and 47th in profits according to the *Globe and Mail*'s survey of the top 1000 companies in Canada.

To some extent, though, the Canadian Pacific has become simply another large Canadian corporation. The various companies have about 127,000 employees and 62,000 shareholders. CPE owns a major part of over 150 companies and has interests in over 100 more. One story claims that during negotiations with a union, company officials failed to report the profits from a line which CPR owned – they had forgotten about it!

The Company's activities extend into the US, Greenland, Spain, Australia and South Africa among other places. At the end of the last century, it acquired a small mining company to provide traffic for a branch line in British Columbia and to rid the region of a man who might have proved a nuisance to the Company. Then it acquired smelters, and in time Consolidated Mining and Smelting (Cominco) came into existence as a major Canadian base metal producer. In 1961, the Canadian Government, bent on developing the north at any cost and employing its native people, built a railway to Pine Point in the Mackenzie District of the Northwest Territories. The majority interest in the mine belonged to Cominco. But it was Canadian National, the railway line that built and operated the highly profitable mine. Ore from Pine Point went to the Cominco smelter at Trail as nearby deposits were exhausted. The mine shut down temporarily in 1982, a victim of poor lead-zinc prices and international competition.

Opposite: The *Dayliner* builds up speed outside the town of Ellerslie on the Alberta prairie.
Below: The CPR *Dayliner* makes the Calgary to Edmonton run, taking on passengers at Wetaskiwin, Alberta.

Red locomotive 1802 idles on a snowy day in North Bay, Ontario. This E-8 unit is one of only three diesel-electrics specifically designed as passenger units. The 1800s operate out of Montrēal.

In 1955, the CPR introduced the scenic-domed, stainless steel passenger train, *The Canadian,* on its run between Montreal/Toronto and Vancouver. But the Company realized that it could no longer make money on passengers. In a presentation to the MacPherson Commission on Transportation in 1960, CPR vice-president Robert Emerson stated that the railway planned to scrap $64 million worth of passenger equipment. He doubted 'whether it is fully realized the extent to which Canadian Pacific is a freight road . . . passenger train service on Canadian Pacific is no longer required for the economic well being of Canada.' In 1973, passengers on the Dominion Atlantic, a CPR subsidiary that had once thrilled local people with its dark red, gold-trimmed locomotives, had to sign a curious document stating that they were travelling at their own risk between Windsor and Truro. Their train took 2½ hours to cover 59 miles, while they sat or stood in the caboose at the end of a freight train.

Save for some lucrative commuter services, CP Rail left its passengers to be cared for by the state in January 1977 when VIA Rail came into being. By October this new state-owned transportation corporation had acquired most of CP Rail's passenger equipment for $18 million. But Canadian Pacific still owned the tracks over which VIA's trains ran and leased them to the corporation. It also maintained ownership of stations. In 1984 the federal minister of transport announced that the government would be purchasing these stations from Canadian Pacific.

In the same year, CP Rail announced that it would eliminate cabooses on trains – and the conductors. Electronic devices could do their job just as well. Predictably, the unions objected at this increased substitution of machines for men.

The Company has been quick to grasp at new technology to improve productivity and maintain profits. During the 1960s, the term 'intermodal' came into use to describe the integrated nature of the Company's activities. Piggybacking had been practised as early as 1855 to carry coaches by train in Nova Scotia. CPR revived the concept in 1957 to compete with truckers on the highways. In 1977 a Company vice-president stated that the average capacity of freight cars had risen from 39 tons to 64 tons in 40 years. The CPR's 100 ton grain hopper cars could be loaded in 12 minutes and unloaded in three. At that date, railways in Canada carried 37 percent of all goods transported – but consumed only seven percent of the fuel used in transportation.

The CPR experimented with winter sailings from the lower St Lawrence river ports as early as 1962. Five years later, when the St Lawrence opened for winter navigation, the CPR built a container port at Wolfe's Cove near Québec, the former site of its ocean passenger terminal. At Saint John, which has the advantage of the 'Short Line' across Maine to the heart of Canada, CP Rail, municipal and provincial agencies joined with the National Harbours Board to move the port into the container business. The Board built a container terminal and leased it to Brunterm, owned by CP Rail and a private company. The decline in general cargo tonnage out of Saint John was offset by the increase in container traffic in 1970 and 1971. Containers swing from the decks of ships on to rail cars, and solid container trains head for Montreal, 480 miles and 18 hours away. With 16,500 miles of main line track in Canada, and 5000 in the United States, CP Rail can deliver cargo throughout Canada and the US midwest. The

A gorgeous shot of *The Canadian,* brilliant chrome against the snow, now in VIA Rail service, continuing a proud tradition.

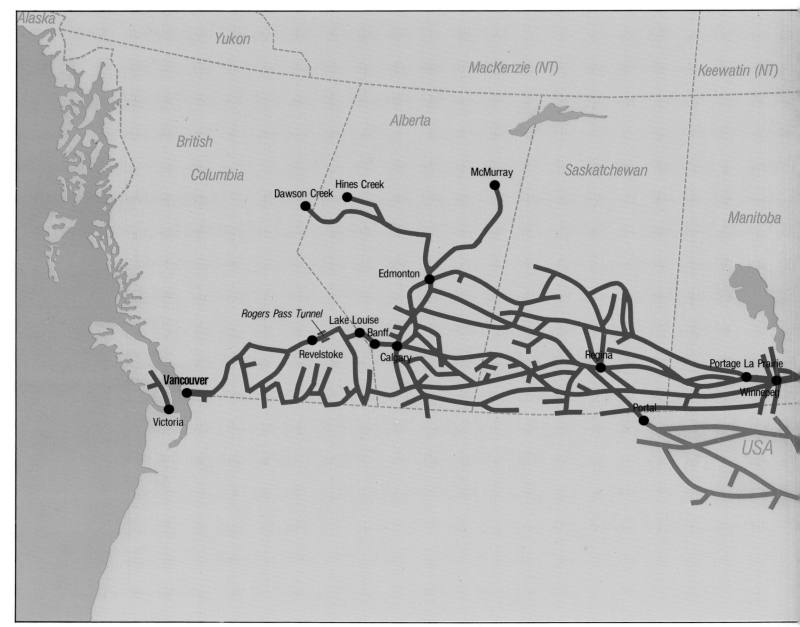

Road switcher 8163 as seen in July 1976 (below) with the old CPR colors, and one year later (opposite) with the new 'action red' scheme.

Canadian Pacific Rail Activities

━━━━━━━━ Canadian Pacific (CP Rail)
━━━━━━━━ Soo Line

The CP Rail system is single track except for the section between Portage La Prairie and Thunder Bay, and trackage in and around the cities of Vancouver, Sudbury, Toronto, Ottawa and Montreal.

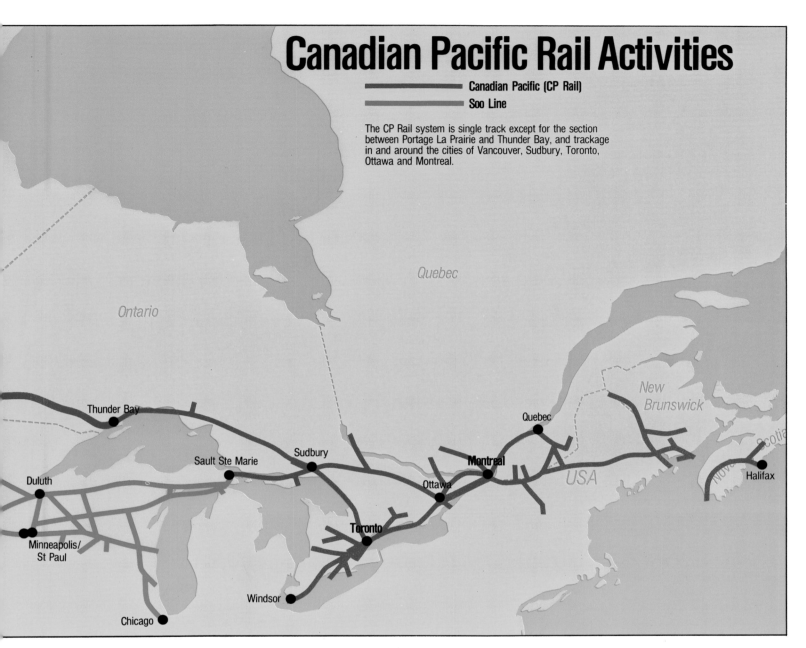

company has developed containers that are smaller and lighter than the standard one but carry the same load.

The Company initiated 'unit trains' in 1967. These carry single commodities; the first took 3700 tons of sulphuric acid to a plant in Ontario. In the same year, CPR Rail began testing remote-controlled 'slave' diesel locomotives for use with these unit trains. The locomotives sit in the middle of the freight cars, and respond to radio signals. In 1968 and 1969, the Company's subsidiary, Fording Coal, together with Kaiser Resources Ltd began to ship millions of tons of coking coal to Japan. Unit trains, hauled by 3000 horsepower loco-motives pulled 88 hopper cars between the coal fields in the Kootenay region and the deep-sea bulk terminal at Roberts Bank, south of Vancouver.

The Company's Public Relations Department issues a sheet which lists the dates of the significant achievements and events associated with the railway. Not unexpectedly, the list fails to include the date in November 1979, when a CPR freight with cars containing toluene, propane and chlorine derailed and caught fire in the Toronto suburb of Mississauga. About 250,000 people had to leave their homes. The evacuation was carried out in a calm and efficient manner, but the Company was still sorting through damage claims in 1984.

The derailment resulted from a 'hot box' – a bearing overheating where the wheel joined the axle. Most freight cars are now equipped with ball and roller bearings that prevent this problem. And electronic scanners at 25-kilometre intervals pick up any 'hot boxes' and warn the enginemen.

In November 1983, after a long debate, the Western Grain Transportation Act cleared Parliament. It achieved a goal towards which the CPR had long struggled – the abolition of the Crow Rate. For years the Company had lost money by carrying grain at rates below those charged in 1897. Under the new system, the Federal Government will pay the rail-ways a 'Crow Benefit' which will reach about $650 million a year by the 1986/87 crop year. The government will also pay the railways for any cost increases for the movement of grain over and above designated percentage increases borne by shippers. Thus while grain growers and shippers complain that the end of the Crow means economic disaster for them, they will simply be paying a more reasonable tariff to have their crops exported. The government of Canada, or, more correctly the Canadian taxpayers, will still be subsidizing the carriage of grain to markets by a state railway and a privately-owned one.

The abolition of the Crow and the provision of greater incentives for moving grain to market meant that CP Rail has been able to raise capital to improve its system. It is upgrading its track, acquiring new equipment, building new facilities. And it is undertaking the largest single project since the original transcontinental line was built a hundred years ago. When 'Hell's Bells' Rogers discovered the pass named after him and received his $5000 bonus, neither he nor any of the Syndicate could have realized how much money it would cost to keep the trains running through Rogers Pass.

The Rogers Pass project now under way will cost $600 million, and be completed in late 1988. It involves the con-struction of about ten miles of tunnel through two mountains, the building of six new bridges, and the addition of 20 miles of second track through the Selkirks.

The project will employ 800 people. Where it took hundreds of men to lay track on the original line, a machine

Left: Mt Ogden towers over diesel locomotives at Field, British Columbia, on the CPR main line, just west of Lake Louise.
Bottom left: Long strips of 1440-foot continuous welded rail are being laid near Revelstoke, BC.
Below: CP Rail diesel locomotives haul the big gondolas of Canadian Pacific's Fording Coal subsidiary.
Bottom right: A CPR freight train stops at the quaint old Lloydminster station on a sunny April day in 1978.

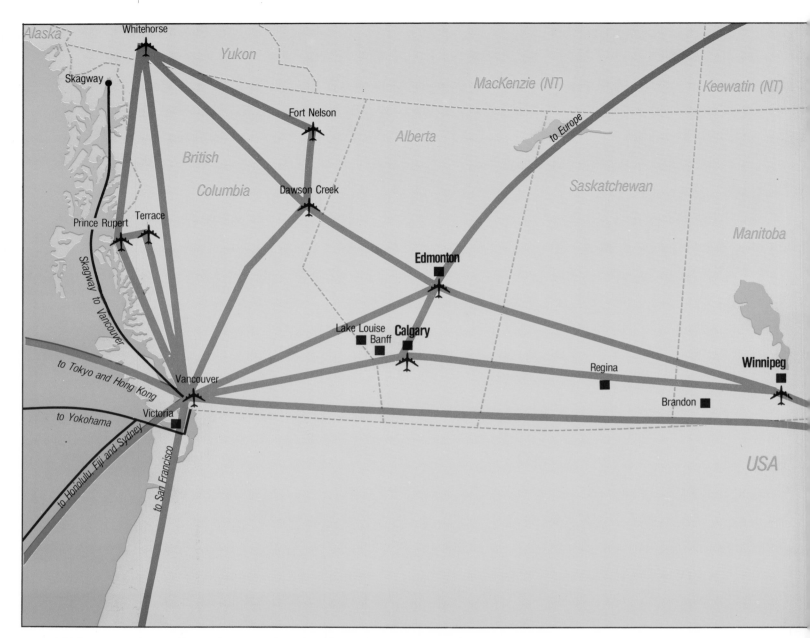

Canadian Pacific Non-Rail Activities

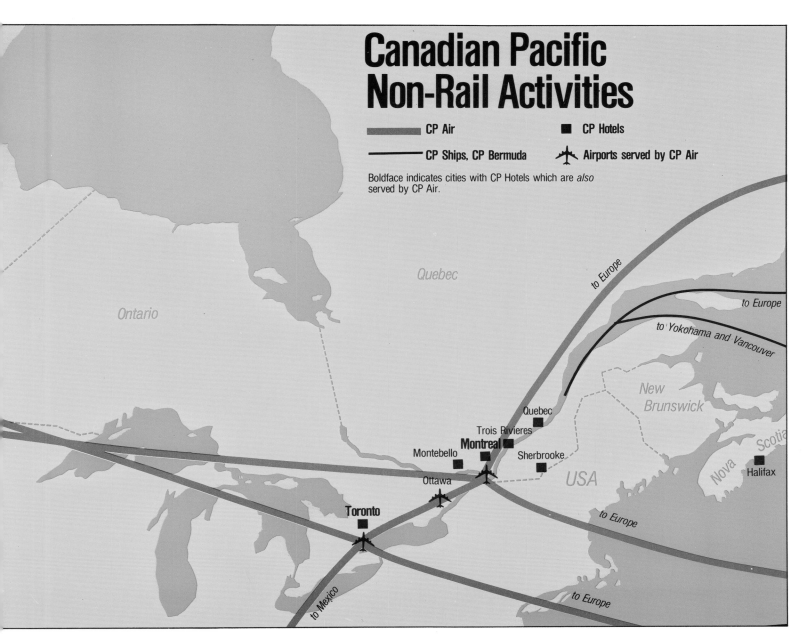

- ━━━ CP Air
- ━━━ CP Ships, CP Bermuda
- ■ CP Hotels
- ✈ Airports served by CP Air

Boldface indicates cities with CP Hotels which are *also* served by CP Air.

Quebec

Ontario

New Brunswick

to Europe

to Europe

to Yokohama and Vancouver

Nova Scotia

Quebec

Trois Rivieres

Montreal ■

Montebello

Sherbrooke

Halifax

USA

Ottawa

Toronto ■

to Mexico

to Europe

to Europe

Left to right: Some of the more famous hotels operated by CP Hotels include Chateau Lake Louise at Lake Louise, Alberta; the Royal York in Toronto, Ontario; Le Chateau Frontenac in Québec City, Québec; and The Algonquin in St Andrews-by-the-Sea, New Brunswick.

Left: Le Chateau Champlain towers over the Place du Canada in Montréal, Québec. Many of its 614 rooms boast arched picture windows.

and an operator can do it all now. Five routes were examined to determine the most feasible one, and many geotechnical and engineering studies done. Unlike the first time the line went through Rogers Pass, the Company also had to undertake environmental impact studies. Modern machinery will strip away 15 million cubic yards of overburden and 520,000 cubic yards of rock. At present as many as six 3000-horsepower diesels have to be added to heavy freight trains for the nine-mile haul up the steep grades near Rogers Pass. The project will reduce the 2.2 percent gradient to one percent.

The accommodation for workers is a far cry from the tents and log cabins that housed the workers on the original line. Two camps to house 400 workers feature single bedrooms, snow protection and bear-proof garbage disposal. And the wages are better, too. A woman working as a carpenter in the summer of 1984 reported taking home $600 a week, and a formerly unemployed father and son team building retaining walls cleared $1200 a week. The West is again depressed, as it was in 1884, and working on the railway has provided welcome employment for many people.

Even in these tight times, the Company still dreams of big projects – and takes new initiatives. In the fall of 1981, it opened its $162-million Polaris venture on Little Cornwallis Island in the High Arctic, the 11th largest lead-zinc mine in the world. Cominco built the mill on a barge that was towed to

Above: The Polaris Mine on Little Cornwallis Island in the Arctic. Note the icebergs and the buildings on stilts in the background.

Below: Cement roadbed foundation is continuously laid as part of the Rogers Pass project in British Columbia's Selkirk Mountains.

Above left: Hamburg Plaza is one of several CP Hotels in Europe.
Above: Banff Springs Hotel rises like a great castle in the Alberta Rockies.
Right: Le Chateau Montebello, nestled amidst a private 65,000 acre estate, was the site of the 1981 Economic Summit.

the heart of the Arctic. Insurance alone cost $1 million.

As early as 1931 Canadian National and Canadian Pacific discussed merging their telecommunications network, but the formal partnership did not occur until 1981. The two companies have issued a proposal to develop a 'city within a city,' the Metro Centre of Toronto on railyards, at the cost of $1 billion.

But when the Company celebrated its centennial in 1981 and threw a party, it provided only hot dogs and chips for its employees at Montreal's Windsor station. In the same year, the world economic summit was held at the luxurious Chateau Montebello, near Québec City. But the Company will do business with anyone. The Chateau hosted a conference on poverty in 1973.

The Company still has to live with its history – and sometimes to suffer from having too much of it. In November, 1982, the Company received criticism for demolishing its 71-year old station in west Toronto, without municipal or federal permission.

Frederick Burbidge, president between 1972 and 1981 and chairman after that, once claimed that the Company 'made its own luck by being receptive to change and alert to new opportunities.' This approach becomes both more difficult and easier as governments continue to regulate *and* deregulate transportation in Canada. In July 1984 the Canadian Transport Commission ordered CP Rail to main-

tain service on a line between Mont Laurier and St Jerome in Québec, on which it had lost $450,000 in 1983. But the Federal Government agreed to subsidize future losses on the line. In the same month, a decision of the Quebec Transport Commission allowed a freight operation of CP Trucks to expand its operations in the province, and to move into rural areas.

Like many other old Canadian institutions, the Canadian Pacific is often appreciated abroad more than it is at home. The Company packages and sells its knowledge through Canadian Pacific Consulting Services Ltd. In July 1984 the Chinese Government signed a $1.6 million contract with this arm of Canadian Pacific to undertake a feasibility study on the storage, handling and loading of coal into unit trains in northern China.

In a sense, the history of this innovative, ingenious company has now come full circle. Chinese came to Canada a hundred years ago to serve the Company and to build the line. Now the Company has moved to China to help the people there to apply modern technology in solving problems of railway building and operation.

SOURCES

The Canadian Pacific's Public Relations and Advertising Division (P.O. Box 6042, Station 'A', Montreal, P.Q., H3C 3E4) issues a short bibliography, a chronology and facts and figures on the railway, as well as other material. Books on the Canadian Pacific fall into three categories – standard works, reminiscences of railway builders, and recent attempts to demythologize the railway and the company. The most comprehensive treatment of the Company and its operations is W. Kaye Lamb's *History of the Canadian Pacific Railway* (1977). J Lorne McDougall's *Canadian Pacific – A Brief History* (1968), commissioned by the Company, is strong on financial and economic aspects, but contains little on the human dimensions of the railway's development and tends to be defensive. Harold Innis published his *History of the Canadian Pacific Railway* in 1923. It contains masses of data and a number of insights on the relationship of the railway to hinterland development. Keith Morris wrote a somewhat bombastic history of the railway, *The Story of the Canadian Pacific Railway* in 1916, when the Company was at the height of its power. It contains material from a range of sources that are not identified, and the book was reissued in 1981. The Reverend R G MacBeth, an imperialist to his fingertips, knew many of the men who worked on the railway, and produced his *Romance of the Canadian Pacific Railway* in 1924.

The early history of the railway is covered in Omer Lavellée's *Van Horne's Road,* an illustrated account with 460 photographs. Lavellée, Canadian Pacific's Corporate Historian and Archivist, has brought together some rare material and information not found elsewhere. Pierre Berton's *The National Dream,* covering the years from 1871 to 1881, stresses the personalities involved in launching the railway. *The Last Spike,* described as a 'historical novel' in the CP Rail bibliography, tells of the construction of the line between 1881 and 1885. Both books were condensed as *The Great Railway Illustrated* (1972). The two books, abridged, appeared again in a separate volume in 1974, with colour illustrations from the CBC television series based on them. The television series, incidentally, was sponsored by Royal Trust – not by the Company. Books by other writers add a human dimension to the railway's story. P Turner Bone, a Scottish engineer, came to Canada to seek his fortune, and wrote an interesting autobiography *When the Steel Went Through* (1947). D E MacIntyre worked on the railway before the First World War, and included stories about it in *End of Steel* (1973). Ken Liddell, a newspaperman

who died in 1975, worked as a newsagent on the railways. His book *I'll Take the Train* (1977), contains much information on the CPR, and has nice touches of humour. David Hanna, first president of the Canadian National Railways, wrote his reminiscences in 1926, *Trains of Recollection.* Hanna has an odd style and a sardonic, admiring, attitude towards the Company. Allen Gibson's short book *Train Time* (1973) tells of the impact of the railways on a small town and its people in Nova Scotia. Elizabeth Willmott's *Meet Me at the Station* recaptures the feel of the railway stations, and their role in community life in Ontario.

Two biographies of key people in the Company's history deal with them from opposite ends of the spectrum of historical writing. Heather Gilbert's *Awakening Continent* (1965) is a life of Lord Mount Stephen in two parts. The first section deals with his activities from 1829 to 1891, contains a great deal of detailed information, but does not tell much about him as a human being. D H Miller-Barstow's *Beatty of the CPR* (1951), an anecdotal and readable account of the life of the first Canadian-born president of the Canadian Pacific Railway, brings this remarkable man alive.

Ronald Keith's *Bush Pilot with a Briefcase* (1972) is a breezy, readable life of Grant McConachie, the man who gave his life to CP Air. George Musk's book, *Canadian Pacific: The Story of the famous shipping line* contains a vast amount about the Company's shipping activities, with details of every one of its vesels.

Robert Chados' book, *The CPR: A Century of Corporate Welfare* (1973) concentrates on what the author thinks the Company has done wrong, rather than on its achievements. Susan Goldberg's *Canadian Pacific: A Portrait of Power* (1983) is as much a study of bigness as of the Company. It lacks a focus, but contains a great deal of useful information, including a list of the Company's holdings and interests. Roger Burrows' *Railway Mileposts: British Columbia* (1982), written by an enthusiast, also contains a great deal of useful information. And E J Hart's *The Selling of Canada: The CPR and the Beginnings of Canadian Tourism* (1983) shows how the Company set the style for Canadian tourism – and created an image of Canada. It also rescues from obscurity that remarkable man, John Murray Gibbon.

Left: The Canadian crosses Stoney Creek Bridge in August 1957, when CPR still had the passenger route.
Top: The caboose in the sunset signals the end of this telling of the CPR story.

Rogers Pass Ventilation System

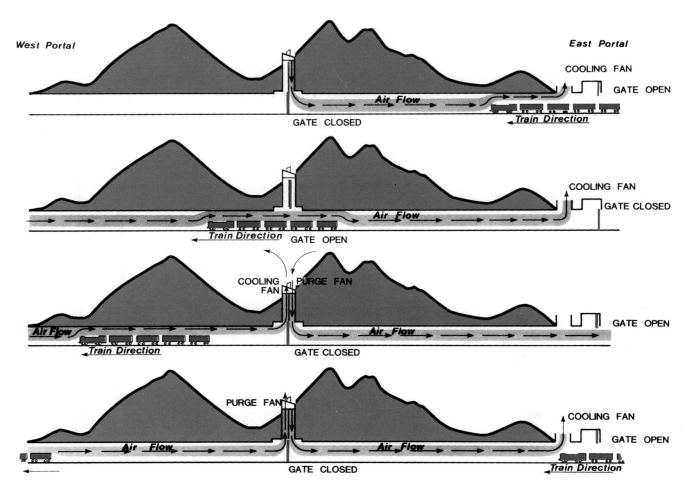

West Portal

East Portal

COOLING FAN

GATE OPEN

Air Flow

GATE CLOSED

Train Direction

COOLING FAN

GATE CLOSED

Air Flow

Train Direction GATE OPEN

COOLING FAN   PURGE FAN

GATE OPEN

Air Flow

Air Flow

Train Direction GATE CLOSED

PURGE FAN

COOLING FAN

GATE OPEN

Air Flow

Air Flow

GATE CLOSED

Train Direction

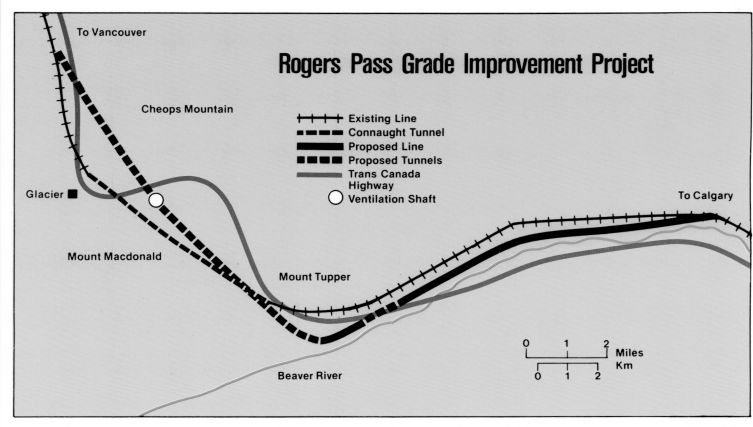

Rogers Pass Grade Improvement Project

To Vancouver

Cheops Mountain

Glacier ■

Mount Macdonald

Mount Tupper

To Calgary

Beaver River

├┼┼┼┼┤ Existing Line
▬ ▬ ▬ Connaught Tunnel
▬▬▬ Proposed Line
■ ■ ■ Proposed Tunnels
▬▬▬ Trans Canada Highway
○ Ventilation Shaft

0   1   2   Miles
0   1   2   Km

Rogers Pass Long Tunnel Cross Section

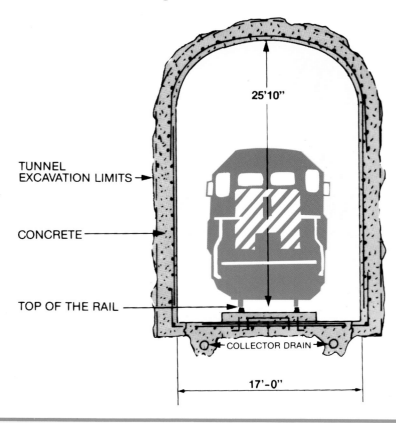

TUNNEL
EXCAVATION LIMITS →

25'10"

CONCRETE —

TOP OF THE RAIL —

← COLLECTOR DRAIN

17'-0"

Top: Tunnelling proceeds at the end of the 268-metre (880-foot) box which forms the west portal of the Mt Macdonald Tunnel in CP Rail's Rogers Pass Project. The tubular device at right is a ventilator.
Above: Another view of the west portal shows the Trans-Canada Highway and above it, Mt Cheops, no longer a barrier to the passage of trains.

Index